C000192696

Smuggling in Devon
1700–1850

Also available:

Smuggling
in Devon
and Cornwall

1700–1850

MARY WAUGH

COUNTRYSIDE BOOKS
NEWBURY, BERKSHIRE

FIRST PUBLISHED 1991
© Mary Waugh 1991

Countryside Books
3 Catherine Road
Newbury, Berkshire

ISBN 1 85306 113 1

The cover illustration *Beach Landing*
is from a drawing by Edward Dowden

Designed by Mon Mohan
Produced through MRM Associates Ltd., Reading
Typeset in England by Acorn Bookwork, Salisbury, Wiltshire
Printed in England by J.W. Arrowsmith Ltd., Bristol

Contents

Acknowledgements

Among the large number of people who have helped me in writing this book I wish particularly to thank:

The members of staff of the Cornish Studies Library and the Institute of Cornish Studies at Redruth, the Cornwall Record Office and the Royal Institution of Cornwall at Truro, the Customs & Excise Library in London, the Devon & Exeter Institution, the Exeter Record Office & West Country Studies Library at Exeter and the Public Record Office at Kew.
Clive Carter
H L Douch
R R M Gendall
Peter Pool
David Starkey

Introduction

'There are many thousands of sailors employed in this illicit traffick, most of whom are victualled and cloathed, and their vessels repaired in foreign countries, who would otherwise become fishermen, and useful members of the community, thereby greatly enriching the sea coasts. . . . The smuggling-cutters are not only large, full of men and well armed, but so well constructed for sailing, that seldom one of them is captured in a year . . . whilst great numbers are employed in removing smuggled goods from one part of the country to another. The smugglers pay for the articles which they buy either with cash, or by the illicit exportation of English wool . . . an injury to the staple commodity of the kingdom. . . .
    Smuggling is arrived to a height unprecedented in this or (perhaps) in any other nation in Europe.'

This is how George Bishop described the situation in 1783, in his *Observations, Remarks & Means to prevent Smuggling*. He went on to estimate the numbers involved as 60,000 of the youngest and ablest men, and 100,000 women and children who acted as hawkers and distributed the contraband. Moreover, a fifth of all the horses in the country were kept for this purpose. In what can have been little more than an inspired guess he wrote that 4 million gallons of gin and almost 11 million pounds of tea were among items brought in illegally in a single year, causing the Revenue to lose £3 million.

The smugglers themselves viewed this from a different perspective. They called themselves free traders, and while prudently seeking anonymity, were proud to provide what they regarded as a 'service' by offering for sale a range of goods at well below the legal price, or items otherwise unobtainable. All contemporary accounts stressed the huge extent of an industry which distributed goods to all parts of the kingdom with cheerful disregard for law and order. It is generally agreed that at times at least one quarter of the kingdom's overseas trade was being carried on illegally. Devon and Cornwall may have been inconveniently remote from London and other major markets for contraband, but

7

they had the great advantage of coasts facing onto two vital trade routes, innumerable secluded coves and landing beaches, and a long tradition of fishing and shipbuilding. Earlier generations had taken part in piracy and privateering. The pillaging of wrecks was an unhappy but understandable result of the harshness of life, when a labouring man could hope to earn no more than 8 or 10 shillings a week when in work. Smuggling offered the possibility of an escape from poverty, a way of using abilities and initiative, a source of excitement, a means to hit back at an unjust society, or at the very least, the consolations of alcohol. No wonder it was so widely practised! And since smuggled goods might cost no more than half or two thirds their legal equivalent, all levels of society were eager to buy. The violence, intimidation and general lawlessness were conveniently forgotten.

Smuggling in Devon and Cornwall was probably not on quite the scale of that in Kent, Sussex or Hampshire, nor was it as violent, but it was extremely important and remained so after the preventive services had largely suppressed the trade elsewhere in southern England. The natural trade links were with western France, and the greatest item was usually French Cognac (familiarly known as Cousin Jackie). Official estimates in the 1780s suggest that half of all the brandy being smuggled into England and Wales came in along the coasts of Devon and Cornwall. Rum and gin were also available, though nowhere near so important. By the same estimates, Devon and Cornwall were responsible for just over one quarter of all the contraband tea entering the country during the 18th century, while in the 19th century smuggled tobacco assumed greater importance. It was also believed in 1780 that 63 ships, or one quarter of all the smuggling vessels in England and Wales, were based in these two counties. Another 50 smuggling vessels were based in Ireland and dominated trade in the Bristol Channel.

The story which emerges from contemporary accounts in newspapers or the correspondence between the Board of Customs in London and their employees at the major ports reveals courage and skill on both sides of the prolonged struggle between the smugglers and the preventivemen. The West Country smugglers were less violent and wantonly cruel

8

than the gangs in Kent and Sussex, but they were no romantic heroes, nor did they deserve to be called 'the gentlemen'. To have actively opposed the free trade when nearly everyone supported it must have demanded real courage and devotion to duty! This book aims to set out what is known of the smuggling story in Devon and Cornwall, shorn of romantic notions, and for those who may be interested, where to go to see authentic sites associated with the trade.

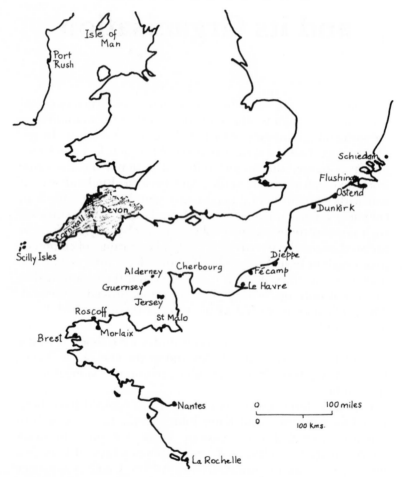

Major overseas supply bases serving the smuggling trade.

1
The Free Trade
and its Organisation

Anyone tempted to walk through the Customs Green Channel
carrying more than is allowed will know that the main motive
for smuggling is money, either making it or saving it. In the
days before Income Tax was invented, much less the Community Charge, the major source of national income came
from taxes on overseas trade. And because England was at
war with her continental neighbours (and later her American
colonies) for so much of the 18th and early 19th centuries,
such taxes at times reached ridiculous heights. By bringing in
untaxed goods the free traders could offer a range of commod-
ities at half or perhaps two thirds of their legal price, while still
making so much profit that it was said that they continued to
prosper if only one out of three ventures proved successful.
The profit margin varied as the rates of tax fluctuated, but a
few examples will show just how favourable to the trade the
situation could be. In broad terms duties were especially high
around 1740, in the early 1780s and at the end of the Napoleonic Wars, providing particular stimulus to smuggling at
these times.

Customs duties on items imported or exported have been
levied for centuries, and King John was the first monarch to
attempt to centralise the system. From that time the taxes
levied on trade proliferated, and a bureaucracy of Customs
officials grew up to administer the system. Geoffrey Chaucer
and Sir Richard Whittington were two well-known men who
served in the Customs in medieval London. It was not simply
a question of the tax charged on a particular item; there were
also prohibitions. To make collection easier, trade was restricted to recognised ports (a system which still applies), and
to protect the English wool industry, raw wool exports were

11

rigidly restricted and heavily taxed. As a result, the sheep farmers of Romney Marsh and similar areas had a huge incentive to arrange quiet and inconspicuous shipments across the Channel the moment the sheep had been shorn. In this way what became known as the owling trade was born, and the smuggling out of wool from East Anglia and the south-east created the contacts and the wealth which was later to finance the smuggling in of a whole range of desirable items. The government reacted by making the illegal export of wool a capital offence in 1662 and for some years thereafter. In a further attempt to enforce this control, in 1699 teams of Riding Officers were appointed to patrol the most vulnerable coasts – the first organised band of preventive men. In addition a small number of Revenue vessels patrolled offshore. The owling trade was never a major feature of the West Country, but it certainly took place in parts of Devon, and Exeter was very important for the manufacture of woollen cloth throughout the 18th century. Instead it was the illegal export of tin and copper which proved impossible to control.

The trade in tin between Cornwall and the Mediterranean countries goes back to prehistoric times, tin being a vital ingredient in the making of bronze. The mineral wealth of Cornwall and parts of Devon arises from the local geology. When the huge masses of igneous, or fire-formed granite were injected into the surrounding rocks, the latter were baked and fissured, allowing mineralised vapours to condense into ore deposits. Characteristically these ores occur in veins dipping steeply down from the surface, often with tin ores near the base and copper lodes higher up. The Duchy of Cornwall, created in 1337 by Edward I, had been given the right to buy all tin offered for sale. Accordingly until 1838 all tin had to be brought to the stannary towns (originally Totnes, Saltash and Lostwithiel in Cornwall, Tavistock, Ashburton and Chagford in Devon) where the ingots were weighed and a corner (coing) struck off for testing, before the so-called coinage dues were paid. Plympton, Helston, Truro and Penzance later became stannary towns, but meanwhile unstamped ingots of tin and copper were regularly shipped out, often under barrels of pilchards.

12   Early tin working was done by streaming, which involved

washing the heavier tin ore from the surrounding gravels, where millenia of water erosion had left these deposits. But during the 18th century deep mining was developed, and this too had significance for the smugglers. Some mines had a labour force of a thousand men, creating a local market for the spirits so readily brought in. Many of the mines were close to the coast, and the shafts and adits (for drainage) provided ready-made hiding places. Deep mines meant a need for better pumping engines and new forms of transport, which led to engineering innovations typified by the work of Richard Trevithick, and as the Industrial Revolution gathered pace, increased wealth meant more scope for the free trade. So whereas the main markets for contraband elsewhere in southern England were in London or the newly industrialised Midland towns, most of what came ashore in Cornwall stayed within the county. In Devon tin mining was in decline before 1700, but copper mining became very important in the 19th century, when Devon Great Consols near Tavistock was for a time the largest copper mine in the world.

Avoidance of Customs duties and restrictions was only part of the story: there was also Excise Duty, payable on a wide range of goods and administered by the separate force of Excise Officers (the Customs and Excise were not amalgamated until 1909). This tax originated as a means of raising essential additional revenue during the Civil War. It was initially levied on goods manufactured within the kingdom, such as beer, malt, candles, salt and leather, but was later extended to cover some imported goods. The main task of Excisemen was to visit public houses and other workplaces to check that appropriate tax was being paid, and Robert Burns worked in this service. Since some imported items paid Excise Duty, the officers also checked at the ports, and their work was assisted by a number of Excise vessels which patrolled at sea. Both the Customs officials and the Excisemen were therefore involved in seizing contraband and pursuing smugglers, often at pathetically small salaries and with meagre compensation for injury. Because the main incentive for their work was the prize money earned by a capture, the two services were often in competition rather than helping one another. Theoretically both the Navy and the Army could be

13

called on to help re-establish law and order, but in practice neither service offered great assistance, and there is plenty of evidence that naval vessels took part in smuggling on their own account!

It was the high levels of both Customs and Excise duties throughout the 18th century which led to the huge development of the free trade. This burden of tax was due to the prolonged periods of warfare, particularly the Seven Years War 1756–1768, the War of American Independence 1775–1783, and the Napoleonic Wars, which lasted almost without a break from 1793 to 1815. From the smugglers' point of view the profitability of particular items depended on the duty payable. The goods most commonly offered were luxuries: tea (a luxury in 1700), spirits, tobacco, fine fabrics and fashionable clothes. The East India Company held a monopoly on the legal trade in tea, and after 1724 tea had to be stored in bonded warehouses until duties were paid. Depending on its quality, tea for smuggling could be bought from continental suppliers at 6d or one shilling a pound, and could then be sold in England for six or seven times this amount, which was still below the cheapest legally imported product. It was said that two thirds of all the tea drunk had been smuggled. The duties were especially high around 1740 when 3,000,000 lbs was thought to be smuggled, and again around 1780 when perhaps 7,000,000 lbs came in illegally. Then in 1784 Pitt cut the duty from 125 per cent to 12½ per cent in a bid to regularise the trade. At a stroke this removed most of the incentive for tea smuggling. Previously it had been the ideal product – high in value, relatively low in weight and (since it came ready packed in waterproof containers) easy to transport. Official estimates in 1883 suggest that 26 per cent of all the smuggled tea entering England and Wales came in along the shores of Devon and Cornwall. Tea was also easy to adulterate, and the Wimborne area of Dorset apparently specialised in the preparation of what was known as smouch. According to the *Exeter Flying Post* leaves from elder and ash trees were left to wither in a barn for some days and then wet with water in which sheep's dung had been steeped (to make it green, rotten and stinking!). It was then spread out to dry, crisped up in the oven and sifted, before being sent to the local expert for mixing with the genuine article (a hideous thought!).

The profitability of tobacco smuggling, and bringing in of tobacco stalks for snuff was often even greater, and the motive continues right to the present day. According to Neville Williams, at a time when the duty was 1/3d per pound, tobacco from the Netherlands which had cost 3d per pound to purchase and 5½d to transport, including freight and insurance, could then be sold to an English manufacturer at 1/7d, leaving a clear profit of 10½d per pound on the outlay. Tobacco duties were much higher during the Napoleonic Wars, and at times tobacco bought for £10 in the Netherlands port of Flushing might be worth £100 here. A lot of tobacco was initially brought in legally and paid duty, but was then (theoretically) exported to Africa, so that the duty could be reclaimed, before the tobacco itself reappeared somewhere along the coast! This documentation fraud, based on 'drawback of duty' was widely practised in London, Bristol and other West Country ports. Much American tobacco was either offloaded from homecoming West India Company vessels or came by way of Ireland, where controls were lax. Tobacco was compressed for shipment, and could be prepared to resemble rope or bales of linen, to escape detection. It could also be adulterated; a Parliamentary Commission in 1844 reported the use of beech and rhubarb leaves for this purpose!

Casks of brandy or gin were the stock-in-trade of most smuggling voyages. The gin, or Geneva, could be produced for as little as 2 shillings a gallon in the specially built distilleries at Schiedam and elsewhere, and could be sold for four times as much. French brandy at 5 shillings a gallon could be sold here for five times as much. It came from western France, and especially from Nantes, and was known as Nantz in consequence. In the days when the smugglers expected little opposition, the spirits were brought over in casks holding an anker, roughly 8⅓ gallons, for transport on horseback. When, later, men became the carriers, smaller half-anker barrels (tubs or kegs) were the normal size, and several original examples survive in museum collections. They came fitted with ropes ready to be hung, necklace fashion

15

Officer—Light Dragoons 1793

An Officer of the Dragoons, one of the smugglers most feared opponents.

around the rowboats used to bring them ashore, or sunk
attached to a line in rafts offshore at marked sites, for later
recovery. This 'sowing of a crop' and its subsequent recovery
by 'creeping' with grapnels became increasingly common
once the smugglers faced determined opposition. If the
brandy remained too long in the sea it became undrinkable.
Attempts were made to maximise profits by bringing in
overproof spirits, which then required dilution and the addition of caramel colouring before being sold. Special glass
beads were used to check the specific gravity of the spirits, and

several sets of these are also displayed in museum collections. Drunkenness was widespread and there are reports of smugglers dying of alcoholic poisoning after using a straw to suck raw spirits direct from the tub. The *Exeter Flying Post* reported the death of Thomas Jenkins, master of the *Swansea Trader*, whose body was found at Plymstock in 1791. Apparently he had drunk an anker of gin (at least 8 gallons) in the course of 16 days, and had eaten practically nothing. Spirits were so widely available that even a woman on parish relief had an allowance. The churchwarden's accounts show that Margaret Foot of Sithney near Helston was allocated over 1½ gallons of brandy during a twelve week period in 1755. (It cost 9/– a gallon which implies it had been smuggled!). According to estimates made by Excisemen in 1783, half of all the brandy being smuggled into England and Wales came in along the coasts of Devon and Cornwall. Amounts of gin and rum were more modest, but supplies were still plentiful.

Other luxury items – silks, fine cottons, china, glass, playing cards and fashionable clothing which were otherwise unobtainable here were highly prized, and often smuggled in to order. Others were offloaded from East India Company vessels or packet boats, where the crew carried on their own private trading. Any item which was liable to heavy duty or was otherwise unobtainable was worth smuggling. Salt, which paid Excise duty and was vital for fish processing was regularly brought in; human hair, flower pots, chocolate, sugar and leather gloves also figure in the records.

Before the free trade became fully organised there was a good deal of opportunist smuggling. Foreign vessels anchored outside territorial limits or even close offshore and acted like floating supermarkets. Homeward bound vessels of the East and West India Companies put into Falmouth or hovered in the Channel approaches so that the crews could sell their personally acquired items. The offloading of parts of their cargoes became so common that such vessels had to be escorted up the Channel and into the port of London to limit this practice. After 1718 it became illegal for vessels to hover offshore, when the first of a series of Hovering Acts was passed, designed to cut these losses. But as the profitability of the free trade became more evident, a whole specialised   17 industry evolved, matching its legal counterpart. Manufacturing centres and warehouses abroad were developed to serve the trade, and specialised vessels were built for its transport. Moreover, recent improvements in the design of fore and aft rigging had made it possible for ships to tack into the wind, and so to enter and leave harbour much more easily. The largest 18th century smuggling craft were armed luggers of up to 250 tons, which could carry 10 thousand gallons of spirits and up to 12 tons of tea. (The method for calculating tonnage was then different; figures by the present system would be much smaller, but there is no formula to make a conversion.) Both the smugglers and the Revenue service came increasingly to rely on cutters, often of 100 to 200 tons, with a single mast and a very large spread of canvas for speed. A cutter could sail in shallow water and had a very long moveable bowsprit (which could be brought inboard). Because this bowsprit increased the sail area, and hence the speed, it became illegal to fit this to other than Revenue vessels. The largest cutters could carry a considerable armament and a crew of 100, as well as up to 2 thousand casks of spirits, and 5 tons of tea. Such a vessel could pay for itself in the first year of operations, barring accidents! But by the 1780s, when significant opposition could be expected from the fleet of Revenue craft, smaller and more cheaply-built ships were increasingly used, whether singly or in convoys. Such vessels also carried small tub boats used to row the goods ashore.

Another type of open row boat or gig had been developed for pilotage (and is still to be seen in the Scilly Isles). During the Napoleonic Wars special galleys rowed by up to 20 men, and with a small sail, raced across the Channel by night from the Kent coast carrying out gold coins which went to pay the French troops. Despite the much greater distance, galleys were also rowed from the West Country to the Channel Isles and even Brittany. (There are still regular gig races in the Scilly Isles and the occasional expedition as far as Ushant, off Brittany.) Inevitably in 1721 it was made illegal to build or own open boats with more than four oars, and there were later amendments to this Act. Shipbuilding was a long established West Country industry, thanks to its maritime traditions, and Looe, Polperro, Mevagissey and Padstow were particularly celebrated for this. However, as opposition mounted, foreign vessels exempt from the prevailing penalties were increasingly used, often with crewmen claiming to be Dutch or French, despite having suspiciously English or Irish names! Irish crews and small Irish wherries were active participants in the trade, even as far east as Kent.

As the smuggling industry developed, so the methods used to land the goods changed. During much of the 18th century when the smugglers had the upper hand and could rely on superior force of numbers, landings were made on any convenient shore either by running the vessel onto the beach or by using small rowboats for unloading. Most landings were made in darkness but by no means all. At this stage the main tourist beaches of southern England all feature in the story: Margate, Broadstairs, Deal, Hastings, Bexhill, Eastbourne, Brighton, Worthing, Christchurch, Bournemouth, Poole, Weymouth, Sidmouth, Exmouth, Torquay, St Ives or Newquay – the list is impressive. Inevitably, as things got more difficult, smaller and less accessible sites were increasingly used and new methods were employed. In sheltered waters casks sunk offshore at marked locations could later be brought ashore by local oyster boats and fishing vessels, but this was more difficult on the exposed coast of north Cornwall. Later still, all sorts of concealments were built into smuggling vessels. This was particularly common off the south-east coast, but there were instances of double bulkheads and compartments under false floors among vessels in Cornwall, and tubs of spirit were regularly hidden under awkward or noisome cargoes such as coal or pilchards. Valuable silks and lace were hidden in commonplace objects. In 1766 a Customs officer searching a hamper of eggs from Dunkirk found one made of finely turned ivory and filled with the finest Brussels lace. At Looe in 1816 a French vessel came in with a cargo of fruit and twelve children's toys in the form of carved wooden horses. These proved to be filled with 51 pairs of silk stockings and nine lace shawls! Smuggler Jack Rattenbury brought in lace concealed inside a turkey!

What the more romanticised versions of smuggling fail to reveal is the huge extent of the industry. Though counties along the Channel coast were particularly involved, the trade

19

Smugglers, a print of 1799 engraved by J P Smith, which shows the typical features of a small landing. Reproduced by kind permission of Alan Hay.

permeated the entire kingdom from East Anglia to west Wales and as far north as Montrose in Scotland. The goods were carried inland, often along what is now our trunk road network, with a recognised system of storage and distribution points. At the local level hawkers delivered the goods to order, carrying bladders of spirits, or tea quilted into their clothing. A well known account of this comes from the diary written by Parson Woodeford of Weston Longville near Norwich, who recorded his purchases of rum and gin from the local blacksmith, and the Hyson tea he bought for 10/6d per pound.

The main supply bases serving southern England grew up along the opposite Channel shore and in the Channel Islands. Schiedam, Flushing, Ostend and Dunkirk were particularly important for the locally produced gin, and Dieppe, Le Havre, Cherbourg and Fécamp also had warehouses. Some West Country smugglers bought their brandy direct from Nantes, but more usually the merchants of Jersey, Guernsey and Alderney acted as intermediary suppliers. The Channel Islands lay outside United Kingdom Customs control by virtue of an ancient charter, and though Customs officers were based there from 1767, it was not until 1805 that effective control was established. St Peter Port in Guernsey was the chief smuggling entrepot, with huge warehouses, and many workers involved in making the special casks and ropes required for the industry. After 1805 the merchants moved operations to Roscoff, Morlaix or St Malo in Brittany, and at times tobacco was smuggled from the Channel Islands into France as well as England.

The Scilly Isles also lay outside Customs control, a source of constant embarrassment to the Customs Collectors at Penzance and St Ives. The Scillies were owned and governed by Lord Godolphin, and among other special arrangements, the islanders claimed the right to one third of all goods salvaged from wrecked ships. Pilot gigs from the Scillies went out to meet homecoming merchant ships and it was said there was 'scarcely anything carried on there but smuggling'. The *Exeter Flying Post* reported in 1764 'Great quantities of foreign teas, brandy and other manufactures are daily imported into this kingdom from Scilly, where boats generally intercept all ships passing by there in their course up both Channels, under pretence of furnishing them with greens, poultry etc. Orders were this week sent to Plymouth to station a number of armed cutters to cruise round the islands, who are to examine all boats that put off any ship to prevent more effectively this illicit commerce.' Open galleys were sometimes rowed over to Brittany for supplies, and William Gibson of St Martins, born in 1794, was one who rowed the 150 mile round trip. Again, though a Custom House had been established much earlier on St Mary's, effective control could not be enforced until 1825. Two Customs men were killed in a fight in Old Grimsby on Tresco in 1791. A reward of £500 was subsequently offered for the arrest of the smugglers' leader, James Dunkin, an un-usually high figure for this date. (Piper's Hole, the great cave at the north end of Tresco is reputed to have been a major storage place, and there were others on Sampson.) Once smuggling was finally suppressed, the result for the inhabi-tants was destitution, only relieved by the development of the trade in early flowers.

Coasts bordering the Bristol Channel and the Irish Sea were initially supplied from other offshore islands, particu-larly Lundy and the Isle of Man. The latter was leased by the Duke of Atholl and became a hugely important smugglers'

Open rowboats or gigs, of the type the smugglers used on St Mary's in the Isles of Scilly in 1891.

entrepot for Wales, north-west England and south-west Scotland. Finally in 1765 it was bought by the government and brought within United Kingdom Customs control. Again the consequence for the inhabitants was extreme poverty, only finally overcome when the holiday industry revived the local economy in Victorian times. But for the merchant suppliers the answer was simple. They moved operations to the Irish coast where Customs control remained lax, and in particular to Port Rush, ten miles north of Dublin. The firm of Ross, Black & Christian was one of those which supplied the trade on the Isle of Man. Among those with depots both at Port Rush and on the French coast were John & James McCulloch (or Macculloch), William Clancie, David Galwey & Co and John Copinger & Co (the spelling of the names varies in the records). Much contraband traffic was carried in Irish vessels and West Country smugglers also made use of all these depots. Lundy commanded shipping lanes in the Bristol Channel and had been a stronghold for pirates and smugglers for centuries before Thomas Benson from Bideford added to its fortifications and storage facilities, and even the smaller islands of Steepholm and Flatholm were used as depots for smuggling.

The sums of money involved in the free trade are astonishing. The cargo on a single large smuggling vessel could be worth from £2,000 to £10,000 at a time when a labouring man's earnings might be no more than £20 to £25 a year. It was said that when three East India Company ships lay in Falmouth harbour in 1763, £20,000 worth of goods were offloaded and sold direct to the local population. Zephania Job, the schoolmaster who became banker for the smugglers of Polperro, was sending out £6,000 a year to pay for goods brought in illegally for his small Cornish community alone. The free traders had a reputation for honesty and regularly bought goods on credit. There are references to cargoes brought in 'under insurance' (one wonders what the premium was!). William Hickey recorded an encounter he observed on board a homeward-bound East Indiaman in international waters off the Lizard in 1770. A smuggler negotiated the sale of part of the cargo with the captain, and then paid with a cheque for £1,224 drawn on Walpole & Co, Lombard Street bankers. He then went on to purchase other goods from individual ships' officers, paying them in gold. There is clear evidence to show that London merchant bankers were arranging for gold guineas to be smuggled over to France during the Napoleonic Wars at the rate of £10,000 a week, when a guinea (£1.1.0d) was worth perhaps £1.10.0d in Paris. Not everyone handling these sums was honest. In 1765 the Dartmouth Customs Collector offered £50 reward for information concerning a certain John Harvey who had absconded with £1,000 in bank notes in a brown canvas bag. 'Speaks French well and has a little of Irish brogue'.

The government had long been worried by questions of spying and other unpatriotic acts linked to smuggling. In Scotland where the Jacobite cause remained strong after 1745, smuggling was seen as active resistance to the new regime, and there are instances even in southern England when smugglers helped Jacobite sympathisers to flee the country. At other times escaped French prisoners were spirited out of the country. (Jack Rattenbury of Beer tried unsuccessfully to carry out four prisoners who had escaped from gaol in Tiverton.) But equally, French aristocrats fleeing from the Reign of Terror after the French Revolution, were brought into the country. 'Letters from a spy' in Kipling's celebrated poem is borne out by the records, but this worked both ways, and many smugglers brought back useful information from France. The strange story of John Copinger may be a case in point (see Chapter 9). Napoleon claimed he got the English newspapers by courtesy of Kent and Sussex smugglers, and Hampshire smuggler Thomas Johnston is said to have been offered £40,000 to rescue Napoleon from St Helena.

The whole question of the morality of the free trade needs to be seen in the context of contemporary attitudes. Piracy and devastating wartime raids had been a feature of West Country life during the 17th century, and the pillaging of wrecks continued into the 19th century. Privateering remained a recognised practice throughout the 18th century, whereby privately owned armed vessels were granted 'Letters of Marque' and licensed to attack enemy shipping in circumstances not far removed from piracy. Seeds from tropical plants being sent to the naturalist Sir Joseph Banks were among items

25

caught up in the capture and recapture of merchant vessels which resulted. Jack Rattenbury, the Devon smuggler, for years divided his energies between the free trade and privateering – and put in the occasional legal voyage when opportunity offered! A brief announcement in the *Exeter Flying Post* of 12th September 1766 reported (amongst items on happenings at court and the arrival of a cargo of oranges): 'The price of slaves was exceedingly high in the French Islands when the last letters were received from Barbadoes, which has obliged the Governor of Martinico to wink at great numbers being purchased from the English.' England did not abolish the Slave Trade until 1806, after vast fortunes had been made by West Country merchants from Bristol in particular. Set alongside these activities smuggling seemed a relatively minor sin. Certainly it was so regarded throughout the 18th century at all levels of society. Wealthy landowners, local dignitaries, magistrates and churchmen were only too happy to purchase genuine Cognac and fine wines. In Falmouth, for example, not only the Killigrew family who dominated local life, but also Captain Isaac Cocart, Mayor there in 1739, were actively involved in the trade. The mass of poor people inevitably saw only the benefits of cheaper supplies brought by the free traders. John Wesley was one of the very few leading figures who campaigned fearlessly against what he saw as the iniquities of smuggling on his many visits to Devon and Cornwall. Others conspicuous for their determination to preserve the rule of law included Samuel Pellew, Collector of Customs at Falmouth, and Warren Lisle, who had overall control of the Revenue cutters patrolling the Channel coasts of Devon and Cornwall.

2
The Smugglers and
The Preventivemen

'Observing of the great quantities of tea and other goods that are daily run on your coast notwithstanding the powers granted by the late Act of Indemnity to put a stop thereto . . . excite your officers and get help from the soldiers. . .'

This letter from the Board of Customs to the Collector at Dartmouth, 13th Sept 1737, is a typical instruction sent to the hard-pressed Customs officers and refers to the Act of Indemnity of 1736, which was an open invitation for smugglers to betray their associates. Any smuggler (even one in prison) could win a free pardon if he confessed all and gave the names of his companions. (But if he resumed his old ways he could expect no mercy.) By the same Act, smugglers guilty of wounding or hindering a Revenue officer faced the death penalty, and there were heavy fines for attempting to bribe officers, for harbouring smugglers, for signalling to vessels at sea or for 'lurking' and unloading cargoes from vessels within 12 miles of the shore. As with other Acts designed to combat smuggling (listed in Appendix I) the problem at all times was enforcement.

The primary responsibility for the prevention of smuggling had always lain with the Custom House staff at the legally recognised ports. The Collector had overall charge of each Custom House; he was assisted by one or more clerks, and in the larger ports his deputy was the Comptroller. These senior officials were very well paid by the standards of the time. At Falmouth in 1822 (when inflation had substantially increased all salaries) the Collector earned £500 a year, his chief clerk £200 and the Comptroller £333.6.8d. At a small port such as Gweek, the Collector received a mere £60 and his deputy £47

a year. Appointments to the lucrative positions were generally
a matter of patronage throughout the 18th century, with
unfortunate results in the West Country and elsewhere. For
example in 1738 the Weymouth Collector absconded, fearing
prosecution for debt, and 20 years later the Collector at Poole
was dismissed from the service. John Knill, who was Collector
at St Ives from 1762 to 1782 is generally thought to have been
in league with the smugglers, if not their organiser. Fortunately, Samuel Pellew who was appointed Collector at Falmouth in 1769 was a courageous upholder of law and order.
With his brother, Admiral Edward Pellew, he was personally
responsible for ending the career of the notorious smuggler
Wellard, when the latter's vessel was caught off Mullion Cove
in 1786.

To the Collector's clerk fell the task of keeping the records
and struggling with the accumulated mass of legislation relating to the legal trade. It is his handwritten letters to the Board
in London that provide the main contemporary account of the
fight against smuggling. The stationery order for Plymouth
Custom House in 1799 gives a clear impression of what was
involved:

	£.s.d.
1000 large quills	3.0.0
2 lbs common wax	3.0
6 dozen long thread tags	3.0
6 penknives (best)	18.0
4 dozen tapes	14.0
One dozen sliding pencils	3.6
One ream thick wove plain paper	12.3
8 dozen fine foolscap	6.16.0
10 dozen second foolscap	7.0.0

Seizures of contraband created problems of storage, particularly at Plymouth, and everywhere the Customs warehouses
were regular targets for burglary and theft. The Customs
correspondence reveals other more unexpected problems with
legal cargoes. For example, at Exeter there were frequent
requests to replace damaged equipment, including £8.13.0d
needed for a new wooden beam for the huge weighing scales

used to assess the tax on wool. (The metal structure support-
ing this beam still stands in its open shed on Exeter Quay.)

The Customs officials most directly involved with the smugglers were those operating under the overall responsibility of
the Land Surveyor & Searcher. The Landwaiter attended the
landing of all goods from foreign ports; the Coastwaiter kept a
check on coastwise trade and the Tidesurveyor rummaged
(searched) ships at anchor. The Searcher certified that all was
in order and was responsible for questions of drawback of
duty. At Falmouth in 1822 these officials earned from £125 to
£150 a year. To facilitate movement within the port the
Custom House had its own open rowboat, with four or more
boatmen in the charge of a Boatsitter. These men could
supplement their earnings by prize money, but they were also
particularly liable to attack from the smugglers. A notorious
case concerned the murder of Humphrey Glynn, a boatman at
Looe shot by smugglers in 1798.

To counter what was seen as a serious threat to the economy posed by the illegal shipping out of wool, two additional

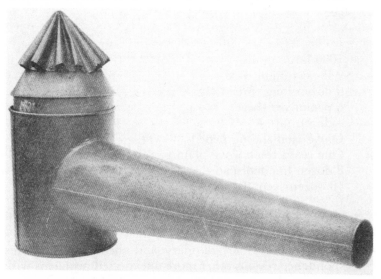

A spout lantern. Made by local craftsmen, these lanterns enabled the
smuggler to direct a beam of light at the incoming vessel by uncovering the
opening briefly.

29

means to control smuggling had been established before 1700. At sea a small number of Revenue sloops patrolled the more vulnerable coasts, assisted by four small naval vessels, and on land 300 Riding Officers patrolled the shores. In Devon and Cornwall the Revenue vessels could not compete with the larger and better equipped smuggling craft until the latter part of the 18th century. The effectiveness of the Revenue vessels increased after Warren Lisle was appointed Surveyor of the Sloops of the South Coast in 1740. For the next 39 years he had overall control of Revenue vessels operating between Portsmouth and Land's End. Warren Lisle is one of the heroes of the preventive services. He was the son of a Dorset Customs officer and entered the service when only 17 years old. He soon supervised the Riding Officers working between Weymouth and Bridport in Dorset, before being given command of a Revenue vessel, the *Cholmondley*. This was based at the port of Exeter, while Lisle himself lived for many years at Lyme Regis. His experience and abilities were widely recognised, and he was later called on to advise both the Board of Customs and the government on matters relating to smuggling. He was sent to inquire into the Customs service at Plymouth and Penzance, and the Collectors at both ports were dismissed as a result of his reports. Finally at the age of 83 he reported to Lord Shelburne (as Prime Minister) on the extent of smuggling along the whole Channel Coast west of the Isle of Wight. After castigating corruption and inefficiency in Dorset, he went on to list the iniquities of Devon and Cornwall. In particular he wrote about complete cargoes of wine being landed in the very harbours of Penzance, Marazion, Newlyn, Porthleven and Coverack 'which must be with the conivance of the superior and inferior officers', and of one large vessel making two trips a year from Madeira on which the tiny amount of duty paid indicated that the whole affair was totally fraudulent. At Lisle's insistence new larger and well armed Revenue vessels were put into service, and for some years private individuals were encouraged to build and equip ships to sail against the smugglers. The incentive was prize money, and the Collector at Exeter was one who took up this challenge. The vessels employed were cutters, clinker-built for strength (with overlapping timbers) and with a huge area of canvas, thanks to a tall mast and a very long bowsprit. By 1782 there were 40 vessels in the service covering the coasts of England and Wales, totalling 4,000 tons and with 700 crewmen and 200 guns. The battle against the smugglers at sea was gradually to prove successful. Captain Frederick Marryat, author of children's books, was employed in Revenue duties patrolling the Devon coast around 1820, when the Revenue craft had the upper hand.

On land teams of Riding Officers patrolled the vulnerable coasts. Each officer was responsible for providing his own horse and patrolling his beat (four miles in the worst areas, some ten miles elsewhere). He was required to vary his routine, to listen for rumours, watch for suspicious activities and keep a record of his nightly journeys. This was a thankless task since the officers were condemned to live among the very communities most dedicated to the free trade. They could call for additional help from locally based dragoons (mounted soldiers), but this was only grudgingly given. The pay of Riding Officers increased from £35 in the mid 18th century to £75 in 1822, but was never adequate compensation for the hazards of their job. The men relied on prize money, whether from seizures of contraband or the capture of smugglers. By the 1780s a captured smuggler was worth £20 (which the free traders regarded as blood money). The journal kept by Abraham Pike, Riding Officer at Christchurch in 1803, has been preserved, and repeatedly records 'no success' on his patrols; perhaps he was receiving suitable gifts! Some officers did give loyal service, only to be killed by 'falling over a cliff' in highly suspicious circumstances. John Hurley, the officer at Branscombe in east Devon died in this way in 1755, when aged only 45, but other officers were far too old for such a demanding occupation. Riding Officers patrolled the more frequently used stretches of the Devon and Cornish coasts until the service was disbanded, but the nature of the cliffs prevented any comprehensive cover. Benjamin Elliot, an officer based at Marazion in Mount's Bay in 1748 suffered a series of misfortunes. The first horse he bought soon died; he bought a second which turned out to be vicious and had to be sold at a loss. His third horse went blind, and a fourth died after a year's service! The Riding Officers of Kent and Sussex had a particularly

31

difficult task, and contemporaries recognised that there was no hope of rendering an effective service 'unless one half of the inhabitants could be hired to watch the other'.

Meanwhile Excise Officers maintained an entirely separate service, mainly concerned with enforcing taxes on brewing and other locally manufactured products. Excisemen could also supplement their wages by prize money, with the result that rivalry sometimes developed between them and Customs Officers over a successful seizure. Smuggling convoys travelled long distances inland, and it was here that they were intercepted by Excisemen. One officer was murdered by smugglers at Liskeard in Cornwall, and contemporary accounts give a graphic picture of violence as contraband landed in Dorset was being conveyed through Salisbury and Marlborough into Oxford and the Midlands, and that from east Devon into Somerset through Yeovil and Bath. There were also a small number of Excise vessels patrolling at sea, and one based at Milford Haven was well placed to harry smugglers in the approaches to the Bristol Channel.

The first signs of successful intervention against West Country smugglers came in the 1780s with the increase in the numbers, size and armament of the Revenue cutters. From this point onwards the smugglers were forced to employ new tactics. Rafts of tubs were sunk offshore for later recovery; smaller, cheaper and faster smuggling craft were employed, and gigs (open rowboats propelled by up to 20 oarsmen) were employed to evade detection, as they raced across the Channel.

In 1809 a new service known as the Preventive Waterguard was established on all coasts. Boat crews now rowed nightly patrols offshore along their allotted stretch of coast, and to accommodate them Watch Houses were built. (Examples can still be seen at Ladram Bay in Devon and Lansallos Bay in Cornwall.) Once the war against Napoleon was successfully won, large numbers of soldiers and sailors returned home, some to take up smuggling, but others to be employed in the so-called Coast Blockade along the most notorious smuggling beaches of Kent and Sussex. The idea had been put to the Admiralty by Captain McCulloch in 1816, and soon teams of naval personnel were stationed in Watch Houses on shore or

32

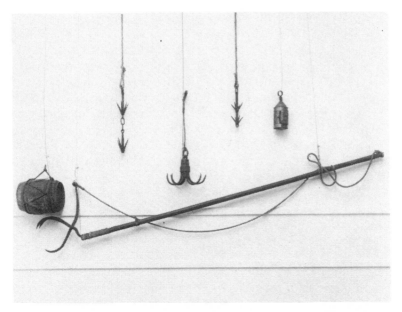

Equipment used by smugglers, including several types of grapnel for creeping up tubs from the sea or shallow ponds, and the typical small keg or tub of spirits.

in naval vessels at Deal and Newhaven, to provide nightly patrols. By the 1820s almost 2,800 men were employed along the entire coast of Kent and Sussex. This expensive and unpopular defensive system continued in the south-east until 1831, but meanwhile in 1822 a Coast Guard was established to take on similar duties along the rest of the British shores. The new Coast Guard amalgamated into one service the Waterguard, the Revenue cutters and the Riding Officers, initially under the Customs Board but directed by a naval lieutenant. Later all recruits were trained at naval establishments and served under naval discipline. From 1831 the Coastguard service took over from the Coast Blockade in Kent and Sussex, and a truly national patrol service operated throughout the whole country. To avoid collusion and intimidation, all men were based away from their home areas, and the characteristic Victorian Coastguard cottages were built as a result. By the 1840s there were over 6,200 Coastguards   33 stationed around the coast of the United Kingdom. Our present system of long distance coast paths owes a great deal to the tracks beaten out by the nightly patrols of Coastguards in naval uniform, equipped with spyglass and when necessary with a pistol to summon help. Meanwhile the smugglers were forced to modify operations further. Foreign ships and crews (largely immune from prosecution) brought the goods to within striking distance of the coast. Vessels were built incorporating various forms of concealment, with double bulkheads or false floors, and contraband was hidden below cargoes of fish, coal or limestone.

The penalties which could be imposed on those caught smuggling increased in severity as the free trade developed. Before 1700 it had for some years been a capital offence to ship out wool illegally, but the main punishment for offenders had been transportation. A series of Hovering Acts were designed to prevent vessels loitering with intent, and boats with more than four oars carrying suspect cargo became liable to seizure and being cut into three pieces. Since the aim was to make smuggling as difficult as possible, the transport of spirits and tobacco in small containers was forbidden. Even on the most carefully watched coasts of south-east England these well intentioned measures proved impossible to implement. Instead the violence escalated, culminating in gang warfare during the 1740s. The Smuggling Acts of 1736 and 1746 increased the penalties to a savage degree. The earlier Act aimed to encourge informers by promising a pardon to any smuggler who gave the names of his associates. In 1746 the names of known smugglers were published in the *London Gazette*. If thereafter a gazetted smuggler did not surrender within 40 days, he was automatically sentenced to death, and anyone turning in such a man was entitled to a reward of £500. Under this Act the Hawkhurst and Groombridge gangs of the south-east were finally destroyed, and the bodies of the ringleaders were hung in chains as a terrible warning to others. In Devon and Cornwall, however, such legislation had limited impact because not only were few smugglers ever captured, but those who were taken and tried locally were almost always acquitted. At worst they went to prison or were impressed into the Navy. Only the worst offenders were taken

34

to London for trial and execution, like the murderer of boat-man Humphrey Glynn. Later legislation softened the provisions of these Acts somewhat and in 1782, when the country was desperately short of fighting men during the War of American Independence, an Act of Oblivion was proclaimed. This allowed any smuggler who could find one landsman and one seaman to serve with the forces to commute a penalty up to a £500 fine. And for two landsmen and two seamen he could go free of any penalty, however great! The Dorset smuggler Isaac Gulliver was one who took up this remarkable offer. By the 1820s the standard penalty for heinous crimes (short of murder) was seven years transportation; lesser crimes merited imprisonment or heavy fines.

It is against this background that we can best judge the activities of West Country smugglers. John Wesley regarded not only those obviously and actively involved as guilty of smuggling, but also anyone who bought or sold contraband, an all embracing definition which must have included almost every inhabitant of the maritime counties. Dr Johnson took a more limited view, defining a smuggler as a wretch who, in defiance of justice and the laws, imports or exports goods without payment of Customs. In fact members of the major smuggling companies performed a range of specialised roles, and there was a significant contrast in organisation and methods between the larger land based gangs of the south-east and the smaller groups, dominated by seamen, in the West Country. The free trade had developed from casual opportunist ventures into a full scale industry by the early 18th century, with large gangs operating successfully in many parts of the country. The most notorious of these, like the Hawkhurst Gang of Kent, faced their main opposition as the goods were carried inland towards their main market in London. Accordingly the emphasis was on convoys of armed men protecting the pack trains, and violence and intimidation were regular features. Arthur Grey, leader of the gang (until his arrest and execution) amassed a huge fortune and built himself a house and bonded store, said to be worth £10,000. His successor as leader was Thomas Kingsmill (until his execution in 1749). During the years when the gang operated successfully they maintained their dominance in Mafia fashion, either by fighting against or taking over rival gangs. We know the names or nicknames of some 20 leading members, and they are known to have met in the Mermaid Inn at Rye to discuss tactics. Few other gangs maintained such a high profile. Most sought anonymity and probably owed their success to bribery rather than violence. In the West Country the larger armed gangs operated throughout Dorset, around Torbay in Devon and Mount's Bay and Newquay in Cornwall, particularly between 1760 and 1800, but we know fewer details about the men involved because they avoided being caught!

It was almost impossible to patrol on shore along much of the rugged and indented coastline of Devon and Cornwall, so the struggle against smuggling took place very largely at sea. In these circumstances it was the superiority of seamanship and sailing vessels which gave the smugglers their opportunity. They were sometimes able to force Revenue vessels into submission and even to attempt to sink them. West Country gangs were generally led by seamen, whether these were family businesses or small locally-based partnerships like those which flourished for a short time at Sennen or Perranporth in west Cornwall. There was less violence, but the records show that far too many preventivemen were killed, maimed or intimidated. Because the groups were smaller, individual members took on several tasks in the business, and there was little sign of the career structure which can be detected in the Kent gangs.

The proper organisation of a full scale smuggling operation required the participation of men employed in a number of roles. A vital first step was the provision of the necessary capital to finance the overseas purchase of goods. A member of the local gentry, a rich farmer or wealthy merchant might invest in a smuggling operation in the same way as in legal trading, or the money might be collected by a group of innkeepers and farmers. In most cases such men remained strictly in the background and their identity is seldom known to us. But Thomas Benson, from a wealthy North Devon family, went on to build his illicit business based round the island of Lundy. His ultimate failure (told in Chapter 10) arose from his overreaching ambition; had he been content 36   with more modest profits, his operations could have continued much longer. Another Devon smuggler, Jack Rattenbury, evidently numbered Lord Rolle of Bicton among his patrons and protectors, and the Carter family of Prussia Cove very obviously had friends (and investors) in very high places!

Given the necessary finance, the gang leader and his partners met to organise all aspects of the smuggling operation. This would involve deciding what cargo to bring in, what vessel to employ, and where and when to make the landing – with alternative arrangements if things went wrong. Typically one member would act as overseas agent, purchasing supplies from the foreign merchants. Another might keep the records, a task sometimes undertaken by the parish clerk. At Polperro it was the local school teacher who became both clerk and smugglers' banker! In some cases the gang leader owned one or more vessels; he might also be the ship's captain and spotsman on whose skilled seamanship the success of the whole operation crucially depended. Harry Carter and Jack Rattenbury are two West Country examples. Alternatively the gang might hire a vessel to make a specific run, especially after 1815, when foreign vessels immune from prosecution were often employed. Whether or not the gang leader was a seaman, he needed to have qualities of leadership and organising ability. Such men held their positions by virtue of skill and courage, and were often self educated.

The lander was responsible for assembling the pack animals, human porters and security guards in the right place and at the right time. The logistics of this operation must have been extremely difficult, given the very limited means of communication. Local farmers had to be warned to allow their horses and barns to be 'borrowed', and the men had to be kept concealed as near the landing site as possible. The posting of lookout men was also vital to a successful landing, with a system of agreed signals. It was usual (and of course illegal) to light fires on a clifftop if a landing had to be warned off. Smugglers also used special spout lanterns to direct a beam of light to an incoming ship, and by the 1820s they used a flink pistol showing a blue flash. By day all sorts of signals were used: whistling a popular song, tethering animals in an agreed pattern, a man riding a white horse, or a red shirt pinned on the washing line!

37

A smuggler and *The Preventive Service*, by William Heath, prints which illustrate the clothes of a smuggler and the uniform and equipment of a coastguard in the 1830s.

The landing party was recruited from local labourers, who could earn more in a single night's work than in a week of normal employment, and might also receive some spirits or tea. For a large landing several hundred horses and men might be needed, some of the men being employed to defend the operation, usually with wooden cudgels or bats, but sometimes with swords or firearms. The remaining men first brought the goods ashore and then carried them on the initial

stage inland. Typically this meant that each man carried two tubs tied together, one on his back and the other on his chest, a total weight of perhaps 100 lbs. Sometimes these men had to struggle up cliffs or as far as six miles inland before the loads could be transferred to pack animals or carts. Whenever possible the contraband was initially concealed some distance from the shore, whether in specially constructed hiding places or hidden among trees and scrubland.

Probably the best example of the various roles within a smuggling gang is provided by the last major group to operate in Kent, at Aldington, just behind Romney Marsh. (It was on this gang that Russell Thorndike based the Dr Syn stories.) 39

George Ransley took over its leadership in 1821, following the execution of a previous leader. He came from humble origins and had spent his early life blamelessly as a ploughman and carter. It is said his dubious activities began after he found a cache of spirits which provided the necessary initial capital. He must have acquired other backers, but we do not know who these were. By the time he became leader, George owned and ran an unlicensed alehouse, the Bourne Tap, and could satisfy the requirements of clients who came from a radius of 20 miles. He met his cronies to discuss tactics at the Pear Tree public house in Aldington. He employed his son as clerk and also as his overseas agent. He retained the services of Folkestone seamen who were hired to crew the vessel bringing the cargo across the Channel. Landings took place along the coast between Deal and Rye, but most commonly on Romney Marsh, and a lookout was stationed on Aldington Knoll in this case. George Ransley's gang was a sophisticated organisation. He retained his own doctor and solicitor against eventualities! In spite of this he and the chief members were captured in their beds, tried for smuggling and murder and transported to Tasmania for seven years. George himself was eventually pardoned and became a free settler there, where his descendants still live.

The best known Cornish gang was the Carter family of Prussia Cove in Mount's Bay. Their story is told in Chapter 8. The most successful West Country smuggler was Isaac Gulliver of Dorset, and since many of his activities took place on the borders of east Devon, it is appropriate to look at his story. He was born in Wiltshire in 1745, but was almost certainly involved in the free trade by 1778 when he married the landlord's daughter at what became the King's Head on Thorny Down in Dorset. This inn lay on the turnpike road from Blandford to Salisbury, a regular smugglers' route. Gulliver took over the inn, and later moved to another at Longham, a key position just north of what is now Bournemouth, but was then empty heathland behind the equally empty beaches from Christchurch to Poole. Subsequently he built himself a fine house with appropriate storage at Kinson, an even better location on the routes inland from the coast. He was fortunate to be operating during the peak years of the free trade, but he was also financially astute, investing his profits in buildings and land, and extending his empire westwards. No doubt he also used bribery extensively; he very carefully avoided force and equipped and trained his smuggling company, providing them with a uniform so that they became known as the White Wigs. He was said to have retained 50 men and had 15 vessels trading for him at one time. By the 1780s his men were operating openly in Lyme Regis, as well as in the West Bay and Burton Bradstock areas. Always a clever operator, Gulliver took advantage of the Act of Oblivion in 1782 and won a pardon by getting men to serve in the armed forces. At this stage he declared he was retiring from the trade, moving to Teignmouth in Devon and limiting his operations to his legitimate wine and spirit business. In fact he continued as before and may well have escaped prosecution (like other smugglers during the Napoleonic Wars) by providing information on enemy activities. William Fryer, a banker from Wimborne, was his financial backer and later became his intimate friend and son-in-law. Fryer's bank was ultimately absorbed into the National Provincial. By the time Gulliver died in 1822 he was both extremely wealthy and highly respected. He lies buried in Wimborne Minster!

Whatever fortunes were made by the free traders of Devon and Cornwall, the men we know most about were much less successful. Harry Carter died in debt, and Rattenbury's adventures were punctuated by a series of disasters. The activities of a small group in West Cornwall are perhaps more typical of what went on. Their ventures around 1815 are known because their agent, Peter Pridham, absconded with the profits and even tried to blackmail his partners. (Papers relating to the resulting court case were found and published by J A D Bridger.) Robert Oats, innkeeper at St Just-in-Penwith was the leading member in this case; he also acted as lander of the goods, together with his brother Thomas. Robert Oats pursuaded James Permewan, a farmer from Trevear near Land's End, to come into the partnership, supplying part of the capital and also acting as clerk. Permewan wrote the necessary letters but otherwise took no active part. Oats then employed Peter Pridham of Brixham as his agent, and Pridham went with the money to Brest to buy the goods from

the merchants Larrant & Co. The captain of the vessel hired
to bring the cargoes from Brest was a Mr Davy, Pridham's
partner. Two cargoes were brought ashore without incident at
Priest's Cove close to Land's End, the first being 480 tubs of
brandy and 200 of gin, and the second 318 tubs of brandy,
plus playing cards, candles, honey and glass. Unfortunately
after this Mr Davy's ship was wrecked and the captain
drowned. Following the third voyage the agent, Peter
Pridham failed to land the goods as promised, and brought
them ashore elsewhere. He claimed that this was due to
unfavourable weather and that all the profit had gone in
necessary expenses and bribes. It later transpired that he had
not fully paid the Brest merchants, so (if it was a comparable
cargo to the first) he had defrauded the group of at least £500.
The innkeeper and his wealthy farmer backer had to accept
their loss, but went on to deal directly with the Brest merchants. Their fourth and fifth cargoes were run profitably, but
the sixth was captured by a naval cruiser off Plymouth.
Finding himself cut out of the profits, the agent Permewan
then turned King's Evidence against his former associates and
tried to extract £500 by blackmailing them. The others con-
spired to discredit his evidence and Permewan lost the case,
deservedly one feels! But the story shows how a consortium of
five members planned their smuggling voyages, brought back
goods costing some £500 in Brest, but worth perhaps £2,400 in
Cornwall on each trip, and lost only one cargo in six.

John (or Jack) Rattenbury's adventures are known because
his autobiography was published in 1837, when he was 59. He
was born in east Devon at Beer in 1778, the son of the local
shoemaker, but his father was already on a naval vessel, no
doubt the victim of the press gang, and played no part in his
upbringing. An uncle took him fishing when he was nine, but
his life at sea began in earnest at the age of 14 when he joined
the crew of a privateer (an armed vessel licensed to attack and
capture enemy shipping). He was excited at the prospect of
adventure and prize money and later described how he was
'like a bird which had escaped from a cage' and added 'I
wished to make a figure on the stage of life'. But his various
privateering ventures were destined to failure. On the first
voyage he was captured by a French privateer, imprisoned in

Bordeaux, and later returned home by way of New York. In 1800 he was captured by a Spanish privateer, and imprisoned for a time at Vigo, but he continued to seek his fortune in privateers off the West African coast, and only finally abandoned this way of life when he was aged about 27. By that time he was a skilled seaman, with a wealth of other experience which included legal coastwise trading to South Wales, cod fishing off Newfoundland, very brief spells in the Navy and, of course, smuggling.

Jack's early smuggling experience, presumably as a humble crew member, was gained on voyages between the Channel Islands and Lyme Regis, and he lived for a time in Lyme after his marriage in 1801. Regular legal employment was hard to come by, but for four years he claimed to have worked as a pilot and victualling ships. He then moved back to Beer and by 1805 (when he was 27) began smuggling in earnest. That winter he made seven smuggling voyages in a new vessel, five of which were successful. At this stage he was involved with the smugglers of Christchurch and Weymouth, but he had also developed the contacts with merchants in Alderney which he was to maintain until the end of the Napoleonic Wars, when direct contact with French merchants was re-established. In 1806 his smuggling activities were temporarily interrupted when he was captured. He chose naval service in preference to a prison term (the Navy always welcomed skilled seamen). He then escaped; (his autobiography lists at least a dozen occasions when he was captured or impressed into the Navy, but he escaped almost as often). Now 28 he had evidently acquired some capital for he next bought a share in an open row-galley for smuggling goods from Alderney, and although this was presently lost in a storm, he was soon back rowing goods from the Channel Islands. Captured yet again and tried at Falmouth, he was being sent with others under escort to Bodmin Gaol when he managed to escape at the Indian Queens Inn, made contact with smugglers at Newquay and was soon back at Beer. His skilled seamanship was now fully recognised and he undertook several legal voyages to South Wales as captain of the *Trafalgar*. But the temptation of more profitable activities was strong; he arranged for the vessel to be fitted with a new (and illegal) bowsprit for extra   43 speed, and went back to smuggling. After five successful smuggling trips, the *Trafalgar* was wrecked off Alderney. Undaunted he joined with others to buy the *Lively* and when she became unseaworthy, the group either bought or hired the *Neptune*, which was wrecked after three successful voyages. Meanwhile the *Lively* had been repaired but was very soon seized with her cargo, leaving Rattenbury owing £160 – 'a great shock to my circumstances' as he records. His first attempt to retrieve the situation was to use a 12-oared galley to row goods from Alderney, but that soon led to capture and a brief spell in the Navy. He then accepted £100 to take four French prisoners who had escaped from Tiverton Gaol out of the country. Caught yet again, he was lucky to avoid further imprisonment.

There followed one of the most creditable episodes of Jack's varied career. Acting as pilot he rescued the *Linskill*, a transport vessel carrying part of the 82nd army regiment, and successfully brought her through the Needles Passage. A relieved captain recommended that Jack should have a hand-bill printed, setting out what he had done, and should submit this to Lord Rolle, the leading landowner of the district. Lord Rolle was very probably already one of Jack's customers, and he certainly became his patron and protector from this time on, ultimately granting him a pension. The Rolle family owned, but did not occupy the magnificent Bovey House, close to Beer, and it is highly likely that this was one of Jack's

'Creeping' – a task hated by the Preventive Service. As shown on this cigarette card, small fluked grapnels were dragged along to hook onto sunken contraband.

depots. Though his autobiography is careful to protect all his associates, we know from other sources that among Jack's partners were members of the Mutter family, owners of valuable storage sites on moorland above Sidmouth (as further described in the next chapter). Meanwhile Lord Rolle's influence apparently led to the withdrawal of soldiers from Beer, which lifted a weight off deserter Rattenbury's mind, as he admitted!

In 1811, when he was 33, Jack took over a public house at Beer and tried to settle down. Unfortunately the venture failed, and after two years Jack was in debt and forced back into smuggling. These were difficult years at the climax of the Napoleonic Wars when smuggling was 'at a stand'. He worked as a pilot, and later when gout threatened to curb his activities, he took Mr Down, a gentleman from Bridport, on fishing trips.

When peace finally came, the way was open for smuggling trips to Cherbourg. Jack was now joined by his son, and bought a £200 vessel in which he did very well for a time, making seven successful voyages. But he was still dogged by ill luck; the boat was wrecked and he had another disabling attack of gout. His fortunes fluctuated considerably; now free of debt his main vessel traded legally, carrying slate from Newquay, but was wrecked on her second voyage. He also had a galley for smuggling from France, and writes about 'a French vessel I had a share in' which came into Lyme. However, the preventive services were now well organised and it became usual to sink the tubs offshore. Some broke loose and were washed up at Paignton, while others were submerged too long and were spoiled. In 1820 we find Jack and a partner bringing tubs back on the Lyme Regis packet boat, and landing these under Salcombe Hill, an episode which led to his going into hiding. The catalogue of his adventures was presently interrupted by a spell in Exeter Gaol. He was set free in 1827 under a bond of £500 and for a time lived a very different life. One suspects the patronage of Lord Rolle was a key factor here.

A plan had been hatched to build a harbour at Beer and link this by a new canal to join the Grand Western Canal in Somerset, and so provide a link to the Bristol Channel. 45

Rattenbury was called to London to give evidence before a Commons Committee investigating these proposals, a tribute to his knowledge of the area and (perhaps) notoriety. For a time he enjoyed an expense account life, but though the enabling legislation was passed, nothing came of this scheme. Lord Rolle then intervened to get Jack a job on the *Tartar* Revenue cutter, an extreme change of career and one glossed over in his autobiography! He became ill (or at least claimed so), was discharged and went straight back to smuggling and a stint in Dorchester Gaol. In January 1836 he was arrested for the last time with a mere 20 tubs in a cart on the way back from Torquay. Two months later he made his final appearance in court to help his son avoid transportation for involvement in an affray on Budleigh Salterton beach. His career was only intermittently successful, but its sequel is continued in the next chapter.

3
Smuggling in Lyme Bay and East Devon

Jack Rattenbury was far from being the first smuggler to operate in east Devon, and contraband continued to come ashore for 20 years after his labours ceased. One reason is that this stretch of coast offered advantages over any other in Devon and Cornwall because it lay directly opposite the supply bases in the Channel Islands, Cherbourg and Brittany, and had the most direct access to centres of population inland – the potential markets of Taunton, Yeovil, Bristol or Bath. Another reason is the nature of the coastline itself. Anyone driving between Dorchester and Exeter will be familiar with the switchback character of the countryside; a plateau roughly 500 ft above sea level is cut at intervals by rivers flowing seaward in deep steep-sided valleys, so that it is relatively easy to travel (or carry contraband) inland, but would be exhausting for anyone to patrol along the coast. Even now there is no coast road, and this section of the South Devon Coast Path is recognised as particularly challenging. In most parts the shore is shingle, backed by cliffs which change from honey-coloured in west Dorset, through dark grey shales near Charmouth, to white chalk at Beer Head, and bright red Keuper Marls at Sidmouth and Ladram Bay. Landslides are a feature of this coast. The most famous occurred on Christmas Eve 1839 when 45 acres west of Lyme Regis slipped seaward, leaving a jumbled wilderness which is now a National Nature Reserve. A lesser landslip in 1790 created the pinnacles west of Beer Head.

All along this coast the sea is steadily cutting back the cliffs and sweeping shingle and sand bars across the river mouths, a process which has destroyed several ancient harbours. Ax-mouth, which the Romans used, and which was so important

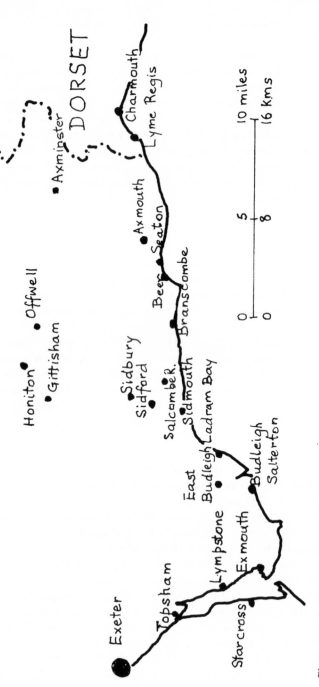

Places associated with smuggling in east Devon.

in medieval times, was superseded by the more exposed beaches at Beer and Seaton long before 1700. Lyme Regis, just within Dorset but closely tied to developments in east Devon, has managed to retain its small harbour, thanks to its famous breakwater, the Cobb. Lyme was a very important port for centuries, and Henry VIII provided money for the repair of the Cobb. The town exported wool, and in 1576 the local population rioted after attempts to tighten restrictions on its illegal export – an early instance of smuggling. The port had a Collector and Custom House staff, and from 1740 to 1779 Warren Lisle lived at Lyme while holding the post of Surveyor of the Sloops for the South Coast, with overall charge of the Revenue vessels.

Sidmouth further to the west had been another significant port in medieval times, but the river mouth was choked by shingle before 1700. However, the town's fortunes were to revive when it became a fashionable resort in the Regency period.

Since Roman times Exeter has been the regional centre and major port for the whole of east Devon. One can still visit the Quay and fine Custom House (built in 1681) and follow the story of its maritime trade at the Information Centre nearby. Exeter was also a marketing and manufacturing centre for wool and cloth, and continued to export wool and cloth during the 18th century, when the owling trade was rife in many parts of England. For almost 300 years ships were unable to reach Exeter Quay because of the weir at Countess Wear, and trade had to be conducted through the outport of Topsham. However, a ship canal was built in 1564 which gave Exeter direct access to the sea once more. Topsham remained a separate small port with its own Customs staff and warehouse, and became important for shipbuilding.

Exmouth grew up beside the deepwater channel at the entrance to the large tidal estuary of the Exe. There was a quay here from medieval times, and a very important ferry link to the western shore. The coast here is exposed, and early sea defences had to be constructed, both at the Point and behind the sandy beach at the Maer. A Customs House was established at Exmouth by 1629, and a Watch House on the Point by 1740, though these buildings were destroyed by

49

storms and had to be replaced. A preventive boat was also stationed at Exmouth throughout the main smuggling period. The town was important for fishing, both locally and in the distant fisheries of Greenland and Labrador. During the 19th century it became a fashionable resort, and Lady Nelson and Lady Byron lived in the charming Georgian terrace, The Beacon.

The smugglers saw the potentialities of the east Devon coast with rather different eyes. Beer and the little valleys opening to the coast between there and Sidmouth were probably the most frequented sites, but the story starts in Lyme Regis itself. Lyme fell within the smuggling territory of Isaac Gulliver and his gang of White Wigs. Though Gulliver's men mainly used Poole Harbour and Christchurch Bay, they were also active in the Isle of Purbeck and in west Dorset. Gulliver had acquired Eggardon Hill near Bridport, an isolated summit rising to 800 ft and had laid out a plantation there to act as a sea mark. It is known that his men used a convenient hide beside the river in Lyme Regis, and within a stone's throw of the Custom House itself.

The unstable cliffs immediately west of Lyme were clearly not the place for a run, but the pebble beach at Seaton was much used, and Rattenbury repaired one of his damaged vessels here. The obvious route up the Coly valley led to Offwell, where various safe houses are known to have existed, marked by bottle ends set into the eaves. The small harbour at Beer had many advantages, and was already the headquarters of a gang before 1760. Its seamen engaged in the lawful activities of fishing and privateering, but also (like Rattenbury) in smuggling. The chalk rock at Beer includes beds of excellent freestone which hardens after exposure. It has been worked since Roman times, and can be admired in Exeter Cathedral. It was cut in vast underground caverns, where the roof was supported at intervals on columns of uncut rock. It is said there was direct access to the sea from some workings, so that small boats could carry illicit cargo straight into an excellent hiding place. Another known hiding place was at Bovey House. This is now a hotel, and stands about 1½ miles north-west of Beer village. For a period it belonged to Lord Rolle, protector and (presumably) customer of Rattenbury,

Bovey House, Beer, once owned by smuggler Jack Rattenbury's patron, Lord Rolle and known as a hiding place for storing contraband.

but for years after 1786 it stood empty. The house had one storage chamber beside the chimney and another 30 ft down a well, and carefully cultivated rumours that it was haunted kept unwelcome visitors at bay! From Bovey House a ridge-way route (now largely B3174) led directly to Honiton and more distant markets beyond.

Three smaller and more difficult landing places lay at the foot of tiny valleys cut deep into the chalk to the west of Beer Head. The beaches along this stretch of coast are still very difficult to reach, and a Riding Officer patrolling here was faced by a series of ascents and descents of around 450 ft. Branscombe Mouth is now accessible by car. The scattered village, where a Riding Officer was based, lies inland at the junction of several small valleys. Contraband landed here could be concealed on local farms (we know that in the 19th century there was a deep pit on Woodhead Farm for example). Weston Mouth below Weston village is more difficult to reach, but was regularly used. The goods had to be carried up 51 the steep climb passing what is now the Donkey Sanctuary, and on down into Paccombe Bottom north of this, where there was another depot. The farmer at Harcombe is known to have taken part. A much more unusual form of concealment came to light earlier this century. In 1953 Mr Clement Ford, Lord of the Manor of Branscombe, showed Coxhead where six narrow diagonal shafts had been driven into the ground in the middle of a field. From skilfully disguised entrances each shaft led down some 12 ft to a chamber 10 ft in diameter at the end. Their purpose was entirely clear! Salcombe Mouth, a tiny combe below Salcombe Regis, was the next secluded landing place. The church tower is known to have been used for storage, despite the fact that another Riding Officer was stationed here for many years. All the surrounding villages took part, and it is said that Sidbury provided the money, Branscombe landed the goods, Sidmouth found the wagons and Salcombe Regis the carriers. Teams of men from Yeovil rode down to do business with this syndicate. The beach at Sidmouth was still an open invitation to the smugglers; when part of the Esplanade collapsed early in the 20th century, a tunnel was revealed leading towards St Peter's Chapel which used to stand behind Marlborough Place.

Jack Rattenbury's associate, Abe Mutter, owned land on Peak Hill to the west, and provided useful concealment in the turf cuttings still called Mutter's Moor. West of Sidmouth the softer bright red Keuper Marls form the dramatic cliffs of High Peak and Ladram Bay, but then fall away to a lower coastline of rocky ledges and low cliffs which continues past the appropriately named Brandy Head to the Otter Estuary and the shingle beach at Budleigh Salterton. Ladram Bay and Chislebury Bay were the preferred landing sites here. Sir Walter Raleigh was born at Hayes Barton, a short distance from the pleasant village of East Budleigh. A less disting- uished seagoing tradition was maintained by two vicars, the Rev Matthew Munday and Rev Ambrose Stapleton, who between them were vicars of East Budleigh from 1741 to 1852. The old vicarage in which they lived is now a private house, but by all accounts this was the headquarters of the local gang, and members met in the parish room to plan their strategy. The vicarage contained many hiding places and secret passages in the thickness of both south and north walls. There is said to have been a tunnel to the church. Bicton House, a mile north of East Budleigh, was the home of Lord Rolle. Budleigh Salterton features particularly in later records concerning rafts of tubs sunk offshore, and was used by Rattenbury. It seems likely that the little sandy bays just east of Exmouth were at least as popular. Stone boats came to the limekilns which once stood on the Maer, and no doubt brought other cargo. According to Robin Bush, the favourite landing sites were at the mouth of the Maer Brook and at Watershott, and the Fairway Buoy was a recognised marker when sinking tubs offshore.

Ranged against the smugglers along this coast in the early 18th century were the Customs officers and the preventive boatmen at Exeter, Exmouth, Budleigh Salterton and Lyme Regis, supplemented by a pathetically thin line of unarmed Riding Officers stationed at Lympstone, Sidmouth, Branscombe, Beer and Seaton. During the particularly difficult 1740s, the Exeter Collector asked for military help to counter smuggling. Accordingly in 1747 a small number of soldiers were based in the most dangerous places. A commander and eight men were stationed at Beer, a sergeant and six men at Sidmouth, four men at Seaton, four at Branscombe and a corporal and three men at 'Tingmouth' (Teignmouth).

In April 1752 Nicholas Boot, the Riding Officer at Beer, reported seizing a pack of wool being carried on horseback by William Cole, who claimed he was taking it to Honiton. But as he could produce no permit he was judged to be involved in owling, and the wool was seized. Two months later Boot managed to capture the small sloop *Fly* and this was duly destroyed at a cost of £1.10.4½d. Then in August 1755 John Hurley, the Riding Officer at Branscombe, fell to his death over 'White Clift' in circumstances which indicate all too clearly the dangers any conscientious officer faced. He is buried in the south-east corner of Branscombe churchyard, and his gravestone (still faintly legible) sets out how he died. 'Here lieth the body of Mr John Hurley, Custom House Officer of this parish. As He was endeavouring to extinguish some Fire made between Beer & Seaton as a signal to a Smuggling Boat then off at Sea He fell by some means or other   53 from the Top of the Cliff to the Bottom by which He was unfortunately killed.' He was only 45 and his annual salary was a mere £35. The coroner's verdict was accidental death. At the same time Nicholas Boot's wife had been threatened with violence, and this led to weapons being provided for both Riding Officers and Boatmen. So a pair of horse pistols and two 'hangers with guards' (swords) were provided for Nicholas Boot at Beer, for his neighbour William Hurley at Branscombe (perhaps the brother of the unfortunate John), for John Colesworthy at Sidmouth and Benjamin Hill at Lympstone. A similar armament went to the Sitter and Boatman at Budleigh Salterton, the Tide Surveyor at Exmouth, the four men stationed at Topsham and the two at Star Cross on the far bank of the estuary. From the point of view of the smugglers, by far the greatest hazards at this time were shipwreck, attacks from foreign privateers or the prospect of being pressed into the Navy. Armed gangs roamed the countryside. In December 1760, 30 horses loaded with tea and 25 men on horseback were seen entering Exeter through the West Gate and riding straight through the city. It was reported that the party then split up, presumably to head for specific markets further inland. The gang responsible was said to be from Beer but the goods had been run in Torbay. Further confirmation of this pattern comes from a report that at midnight on 19th April 1766 Custom House officers saw 40 smugglers and 50 horses, all loaded with tea. Realising that they were in no position to tackle a gang of this size, they got out of the way fast, but poor William Hunt, who had an indifferent horse, was caught and very seriously injured. Commenting that the gang were carrying at least 5 cwt of tea, the report goes on that this was 'the Beere gang . . . whose chief place of rendez-vous and running of goods at present is between Start Point and Torbay. . .' and that the gang readily resorted to violence.

The Collector at Exeter had other lesser problems over ordering equipment and stationery, or how to deal with unusual cargoes. In 1752 he was ordered to take all possible care to stop the import of human hair! Six years later he sought advice about part of a cargo of almonds and raisins which had got wet, and was in such a bad condition that the merchant due to receive it refused to pay the duty or remove it

54

from the quay. It stank and the local residents were desperate to have it taken away! There were recurring fears over epidemics. Some of the crew of a Dutch ship from Messina had contracted plague, and great efforts were made to round up sailors who had gone ashore at Topsham. In 1760 the problem was smallpox, and some Customs men stayed away from work for fear of being infected; the Board in London was unsympathetic over such absenteeism. A more usual problem was the age or infirmity of the staff. Henry Humphrey, Boatman at Exmouth in 1756, had served for 12 years, but at 78 was judged incapable and entitled to superannuation. William Hunt, his successor 12 years later, was injured in a struggle with smugglers. His shoulder had been dislocated but this was not diagnosed for three weeks. The poor man was then tied to an 'apple engine' and his shoulder put back by what was described as 'mere force of the screw'. He was said to be tolerably well recovered; the surgeon charged £4.15.0d.

The 1770s and 1780s saw an escalation of smuggling as United Kingdom involvement in warfare overseas drained the country of the manpower needed for effective prevention of smuggling. At the same time it was being realised that the best

Budleigh Salterton Beach, a well known smugglers' landing site used by Jack Rattenbury and many of his associates.

55

course of action was to intercept the vessels at sea. The small number of Revenue vessels was now supplemented by others built by private enterprise, the incentive being the prize money awarded for a successful capture. In 1743 Warren Lisle's sloop *Cholmondley* of 80 tons was based at Exeter, and an over optimistic Collector reported to London on the success of the Revenue vessels '. . . able to attack the smugglers in every creek and little harbour along the coast of Devenshire and Cornwall.' Lisle subsequently provided two other ships, both called *Beehive*, and William Bagnell provided two called *Wren*. In 1776 the Collector financed the building of the *Alarm* lugger, which cost around £1,000. Seven years later this was replaced by another *Alarm* cutter of 130 tons, with 12 guns and a crew of 36, which patrolled between Portland and Start Point and brought a succession of seizures into Exmouth. For example, in July 1803 she seized the smuggling sloop *Pelican* of Weymouth, with her cargo of spirits and tobacco. Warren Lisle remained concerned about corruption, and in 1782 reported to the Prime Minister that the four Revenue cutters operating between St Alban's Head in Dorset and Berry Head in Torbay '. . . agree with the Smuglers, and content themselves with a small part from the Smugler, suffer the greater part to be run on shore.' Naval vessels were also ordered to help, but this was not an unqualified success. In June 1791 the Exeter Collector reported that a Customs boatman at Budleigh Salterton had suffered ill-usage when a lieutenant and some of the crew of HMS *Narcissus* seized 40 casks and a boat from him! Earlier that year a smuggling vessel carrying dry goods and 100 kegs of spirits was driven on shore near Exmouth in heavy gales. The 'looker-out for wrecks' made off with 10 casks, hotly pursued by the local Customs men!

The peak years for smuggling in east Devon, as elsewhere, were around 1782, when reports from the Commissioners of Excise to the Prime Minister spoke of 25 armed vessels of up to 100 tons, and crews of up to 20 men carrying goods into the Exeter area. They estimated that 1,248,000 gallons of brandy and 806,400 lb of tea had been brought in during the previous three years (no figures were given for tobacco), so that as much as ninety per cent of the tea and spirits consumed had been smuggled. During a single month in 1784 the *Alarm* cutter had seized nearly 1,200 casks, and this can only have been a small fraction of what came ashore. The quantity of captured contraband led to other problems. Tobacco was generally burned – 2,025 lb of it at Topsham in 1770 for example, but condemned teas were usually sent to London for disposal. Spirits were kept in the Customs warehouse (which led to attempted break-ins), and then sold locally. A sale at Topsham in 1787 offered 'in small lots for private family use only' 1,587 gallons of brandy, 694 of gin and 143 of rum.

Two episodes from this time cast light on the regular routes taken to inland markets. In 1787 two Excisemen were murdered by a gang of smugglers at Roncombe Gate between Beer and Honiton (now B3174). A £200 reward or a free pardon was offered for information leading to conviction of those responsible. About the same time casks were found in a pond at Halsbeare Farm, Blackborough in the Blackdown Hills on the Somerset border, an episode which parallels the 'moon-raker' story of Wiltshire. Sampford Peverell, close to the M5 near Tiverton, is also known to have been a smugglers' depot.

After 1800 most of the large seizures concern rafts of tubs sunk offshore. The smugglers had to contend with Revenue cutters at sea and the row boats of the Waterguard patrolling just offshore. These are the years when Rattenbury was bringing goods from Alderney, but suffering some losses through bad weather, or on occasion being captured. The emphasis was on seizing the men rather than the goods, and Rattenbury's chief aim to avoid serving in the Navy. Once Napoleon was finally defeated and war with France ended, the French took an active part in proceedings. French vessels brought goods to within striking distance of the coast, and the contraband was then sunk or brought ashore in small boats. In a typical case in 1819 the Revenue cutter *Sprightly* chased a French row-galley for four hours. The smugglers threw 200 kegs overboard to lighten the load, but were forced ashore and six of the crew were captured. Rough seas claimed victims from both sides. On the north wall of Seaton church is a monument to William Henry Paulson, Midshipman of HMS *Queen Charlotte*, who perished in a gale off Sidmouth 'whilst cruising in a galley for the prevention of smuggling'. He was only 23, and eight other seamen died with him.

Smugglers attacked, a popular early 19th century print by an unknown artist.
Reproduced by kind permission of Alan Hay.

On shore the Riding Officers were recording frequent but
small seizures. In March 1816 the Sidmouth officer seized
spirits from a gang on Peak Hill. He was then assaulted by
smugglers who took back part of their haul, and a reward of
£100 was offered for help in their capture. Abe Mutter,

Rattenbury's associate, hid contraband in his turf cuttings on the moor to the north, so it is clear who was responsible! This was a year when Rattenbury was doing well bringing cargoes from Cherbourg, and able to buy a new vessel, the *Elizabeth & Kitty*. Thomas Wimble (who was evidently Riding Officer at Axmouth) was taking his seizures to Lyme Regis. In February 1816 he seized 170 ankers of brandy, for which he claimed 4 shillings in expenses. During the spring of 1821 he made similar captures in the Axmouth and Combpyne area, but thereafter his captures were much smaller, and included one in a copse near Charmouth. Either he was colluding with the smugglers or the battle was being won.

The establishment of the national Coast Guard in 1822 marked the beginning of the end. Rattenbury was already in trouble, having been sent to Exeter gaol. He was caught again while smuggling at Dawlish in 1825, and went back to Exeter gaol. Then, following his time in London giving evidence before a Parliamentary Inquiry into a canal link between the Bristol and English Channels, he was actually persuaded to serve on the *Tartar* Revenue cutter. He was soon back smuggling with his son, which led to a short stay in Dorchester gaol. In 1833 he made his last trip to Cherbourg, and was caught for the last time three years later, while bringing brandy in a cart from Torquay.

Rattenbury's associates kept up the smuggling tradition. Abe Mutter's brother Samuel now took over the supply side, landing cargoes in the usual places between Exmouth and Seaton. He also kept a public house at Exmouth, and the local preventivemen soon learned that when he was absent, a run was on. He was arrested (not for the first time) in 1843. Abe Mutter's son John was said to be the last Westcountryman to earn his living by smuggling. This story was taken further when in 1930 the *Western Morning News* published the confessions of Mr H Godfrey, an Australian merchant from Sydney, but once resident in Sidford. He had emigrated in 1856 after his father's death. As a lad he helped his father's smuggling activities, and had taken kegs in a cart and stowed them in a deep camouflaged pit. On one occasion young Godfrey was caught on his way to Windwhistle public house with ten kegs. After the final run at Exmouth, probably in 1856, he was returning to Sidford at 2 a.m. with 88 small tubs which he had no time to conceal, when these were seized. Young Godfrey and his father escaped and spent six weeks with a relative in Gittisham (near Honiton). His father was eventually fined £1,100 – three times the value of the brandy. Though he must have been over 80 when he recounted this, he remembered that the brandy came over in a vessel provided by French merchants, but was piloted by a man he called 'W Mutters' who alone knew the landing place. The brandy had been paid for by a draft on a Honiton bank!

Three other men remembered what went on. Henry Northcote, who was born in 1819, remembered carrying tubs up the combe below Salcombe Regis and taking them to a pit in Paccombe Bottom, from where they were taken on by wagon. Harold James Hooper of Honiton told Coxhead about his father, James Eli Hooper, born at Bagwell's Cottage near Offwell in 1859, and his grandfather Daniel Hooper, who was born in 1831. Daniel used to help with landings at Branscombe and Salcombe Regis below the 400 ft cliffs. Ropes were

The quay at Topsham on the Exe estuary. For 300 years, Topsham was the outport for Exeter, before the cutting of the ship canal in 1564.

tied at each corner of a field gate. A man went down on this makeshift platform and sent up successive loads. At one stage the rope broke and a man was killed. Samuel Bray, the farmer at Woodhead Farm near Beer, is known to have made a frustrated excursion to bring back brandy from north Devon during the 1850s (see Chapter 10). His 18 year old son George Bray heard the preventivemen behind him as he was taking brandy (which had been landed at Budleigh Salterton in 1858) up Trow Hill (on A3052), but managed to throw the tubs into a ditch. He retrieved them later, and took them to the hiding place at Woodhead Farm. This was a deep pit behind the cowshed, covered by tree trunks and a rick of hay. The store was never discovered; it seems a fitting end to the tale of east Devon smugglers!

PLACES TO VISIT

Beer Village and Head, Bovey House and The Quarries
(Carpark in village, or larger one up Common Road, on clifftop.) There are a few old buildings in the village, but the beach itself, with local boats, is down a steep descent. There are several excellent walks. A signed coast path westwards starts from just below the cliff carpark. The best views of the whole coast can be gained from Beer Head on a walk to Branscombe Mouth. An alternative route descends through chalk pinnacles of the 1790 landslip. Bovey House (now a hotel) an excellent Tudor building which Rattenbury probably used as a store, can be reached by car at the signed turning from B3174 or on foot up the valley leading north-west from Beer. Quarry Caves in Quarry Lane, one mile west of the village on a minor road are open daily, Easter – end October. There are conducted hour-long tours through ancient underground workings and a museum. Tel: 0297 80282.

Branscombe
The most easily reached of the smuggling beaches between Beer and Sidmouth is accessible down steep and narrow roads from A3052. (Carpark at Branscombe Mouth beside beach and below Coastguard cottages.) A scatter of stone and thatch cottages lies a little inland, with the church at the west end. John Hurley's weathered and damaged gravestone is in the south-east corner of the churchyard and is just legible. Smuggling beaches at Weston Mouth and Salcombe Mouth can be reached either along the South Devon Coast Path or directly from Dunscombe and Salcombe Regis respectively, in each case with physical effort! A small stone house with slate roof on a stone plinth at the back of the beach at Weston Mouth appears to be the old Watch House.

East Budleigh, Otterton and Ladram Bay
The Old Rectory at East Budleigh (private) is on the narrow road towards Hayes Barton (Raleigh's birthplace, also private). The gardens at Bicton, just to the north, are open (entry charge), but Bicton House, home of Rattenbury's patron Lord Rolle, is not open. Both East Budleigh and Otterton villages are attractive, with thatched cottages lining a stream. The approach to Ladram Bay is dominated by caravan and carparks, but the small shingle beach among rose-red cliffs and stacks is most attractive. A small decaying and private building on the clifftop beyond the Three Rocks Hotel is probably the old Watch House.

Exeter and Topsham
Contact Exeter Tourist Information Centre (0392 265862) for the current programme of free guided walks during main season, or go independently to the Custom House and Quay House Interpretation Centre on the opposite side of the river from the Maritime Museum. (No parking on site; easy to combine with Maritime Museum). Other tours in the programme include canal cruises and Topsham. If you are visiting Topsham independently use the signed carpark south of the station and explore on foot. There is a good view of the original quay and Custom House area from beside the church.
62 Walk along the Strand and note Shell House (1571), Broad-

way House (c 1700) and Passage Inn (dated 1788 but older). The museum in a merchant's house is open main season on various afternoons. There are also good views from the raised walkway at the south end of the Strand.

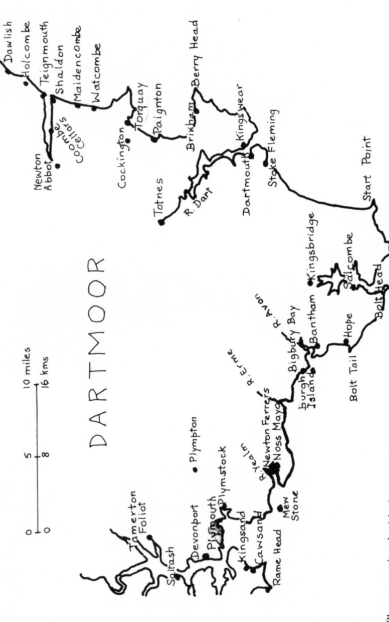

DARTMOOR

10 miles
16 kms

Dawlish
Holcombe
Teignmouth
Shaldon
Maidencombe
Watcombe
Coffear's Cottage
Newton Abbot
Torquay
Paignton
Berry Head
Brixham
Kingswear
Stoke Fleming
Cockington
Totnes
R. Dart
Dartmouth
Start Point
Prawle Point
Kingsbridge
Salcombe
Bolt Head
Bantham
Bigbury Bay
R. Avon
Hope
Bolt Tail
Burgh Island
Noss Mayo
Newton Ferrers
R. Yealm
R. Erme
Mew Stone
Plympton
Plymstock
Plymouth
Devonport
Tamerton Foliot
Saltash
Kingsand
Cawsand
Rame Head

Places associated with the smuggling trade in south Devon.

4
Torbay and the Coast from Dawlish to Start Point

For many centuries Dartmouth was the major trading port of south-east Devon. Its situation beside deep water and within the shelter of the winding Dart estuary is magnificent. It is fascinating to imagine the scene when men and vessels gathered here before setting out on the Crusades of 1147 and 1190. Geoffrey Chaucer, who was a Customs officer in the Port of London, came to Dartmouth in 1373, and has left a telling picture of the freebooting 'shipman of Derthmute':

'Full many a draughte of wyn had he ydrawe
From Burdeux-ward, whyl that the chapman sleep.
Of nyce conscience took he no keep.
If that he faught, and hadde the hyer hond,
By water he sente hem hoom to every lond.'

Untroubled by conscience, suntanned and vigorous he rode on pilgrimage to Canterbury, a dagger at his side! The medieval merchants of Dartmouth did indeed grow rich on the wine trade with France, and later diversified into exporting woollen cloth or minerals from Dartmoor. The town was vulnerable to attack from France, which led to the building of Dartmouth Castle in 1481, and Kingswear Castle on the opposite bank ten years later. A chain across the estuary provided extra protection, and a small fort at Baynard's Cove was added down by the Quay in 1537. The Pilgrim Fathers made their first attempt to sail to America from Dartmouth (but had to return to Plymouth for repairs) and involvement

65

in Greenland whaling and the Newfoundland cod fisheries led
to a second period of prosperity for the town.

There was more than a hint of the freebooting adventurer
about some Dartmouth merchants. Richard Hakluyt and Sir
John Gilbert treated Dartmouth (along with Exeter, Penzance
and St Ives) as though they were free ports, and shipped out
copper illegally in 1580; Spanish wines and tobacco were also
brought in. During the 17th century when piracy was common particularly in the West Indies and Indian Ocean, men
from Dartmouth took part. The harsh conditions of the Newfoundland fisheries encouraged recruitment into the pirate
crews. Stokenham church records of 1581 include a reference
to the pirate Henri Muge, whose body was hung in chains on
Start Point as a warning to others. From 1698 onwards a
Revenue vessel was stationed at Dartmouth to help maintain
law and order, but when the town suffered from outbreaks of
plague, shipping was diverted to Salcombe or into Torbay,
where there was little control of what went on. It is no
surprise, therefore, that the records of 18th century smuggling
start with accounts of villainy in Torbay.

No part of the Devon coastline can have seen more changes
in the last 250 years than the sheltered shores of Torbay,
between the protecting limestone headlands at Babbacombe
in the north and Berry Head to the south. The delightful
sandy beaches here were patronised by smugglers at least as
early as the 16th century, when Leland referred to 'thirty
hoggesheddes of wine in a sellar in Torbay and sugers in
quantities not known'. In the 1760s, when the Beer gang
operated here, Torquay was little more than a fishing village
whose harbour had originally served the monks of the 12th
century Torre Abbey. Paignton and Cockington were other
small villages. Brixham was more important, with its quay
and fishmarket, its fishing fleet and shipbuilding yards, and it
was at Brixham that William of Orange came ashore in 1688
on his way to become King of England. Berry Head above
Brixham offered excellent lookout and signalling opportunities to the smugglers, and there were convenient caves for
storage. One cave is reputed to have been used by smuggler
Bob Elliott. For the rest, the countryside was thinly peopled
66   and totally rural. It was also almost entirely undefended

against the smugglers. All seaborne trade from just south of Teignmouth right round to Bantham and Bigbury Bay was controlled from Dartmouth, and watched over by individual Customs officers stationed at Torquay, Paignton, Brixham and Salcombe, as well as at Totnes and in Dartmouth itself; there is no mention of Riding Officers patrolling this coast. The smuggling fraternity continued to use Torbay until well into the 19th century, and Jack Rattenbury was carrying away his last load from here when he was caught in 1836. It was the Napoleonic Wars which led to the development of Torquay as a fashionable resort. Naval vessels rode out winter storms in Torbay, and houses were built for the families of their officers. The holiday facilities and retirement homes came very much later.

Below the cliffs which run north of Torquay is a sequence of smaller coves and beaches known to have been used by the smugglers. Contraband landed at Brandy Cove below Black Head, Anstey's Cove and Oddicombe beach was evidently initially concealed in the Barton area. One known hiding place was under the hearthstone of a cottage next to Park Road Post Office in St Marychurch. A smuggler called Drake lived in a cottage within a fold in the cliffs at Petit Tor, and is said to have added wrecking to his other activities. The sequence of beaches continues northwards past Smuggler's Hole, Watcombe Beach, Maidencombe Beach, Labrador Beach, Smuggler's Cove and Ness Beach on the way to Shaldon. Known hiding places were at Rocombe Farm, where there was a room above a fireplace, and Maidencombe Farm, which had a trapdoor in a ceiling leading to another secret chamber. According to Coxhead, the goods were then taken down to the Teign estuary, where boats were waiting to distribute these. The isolated Combe Cellars Inn on the southern shore of the estuary was the ideal location for a depot, and it is known that as much as seven tons of tobacco could be stored here. At low tide the estuary could be forded at this point.

Teignmouth is an old established small port which has built boats and handled minerals exported from Dartmoor. In the early 18th century it was still recovering from a destructive French raid in 1690. Beaches here were an invitation to the

Combe Cellars Inn on the Teign estuary, which could be forded at this point. The present Victorian building stands on the site of the original inn where as much as 7 tons of illicit tobacco were stored on one occasion.

smugglers, and continued in use into the 1830s. The preferred landing place was just below the rock stacks called the Parson and Clerk, and a lane still leads up from here to Holcombe village, where there were caves cut into the sandstone cliffs. Near Dawlish the obvious landing site was on the Warren, the spit of sand and shingle which stretches out into the Exe estuary. Again, a smugglers' track led up to the Mount Pleasant Inn with its commodious cellars and caverns in the cliffs above. Teignmouth and Dawlish came within the control of the port of Exeter. The officer based at 'Tingmouth' was given additional help to combat smuggling when a corporal and three soldiers were stationed here in 1747. What finally destroyed the free trade along this stretch of coast was the opening of the railway line in 1848.

South of Dartmouth the great shingle beaches which run round Start Bay to Start Point must have provided opportunities for all sorts of landings. (This is where American troops practised landing techniques before the Normandy invasion of the Second World War.) It is known that one hiding place was

68

Ness Beach, Shaldon where there are two tunnel entrances, the upper of which is an extension to an original smugglers' tunnel.

at Stoke Fleming but no specific records of smuggling in the area have survived. It was the more accessible beaches of Torbay which feature in all the early records. There was a problem over homewardbound ships of the Newfoundland fishing fleets and their escorts, who evidently called in on the American colonies and then unloaded all manner of good things in Torbay. A report speaks of very great frauds committed by the passengers who brought home large quantities of rum, tobacco, salt, wine and other items: 'take care that such ships be not permitted to discharge in Torbay for the future but come into the harbour at Dartmouth'. Attempts to stop the illegal export of wool were a constant preoccupation, and in 1746 there was a strict order to stop arms and military stores from going out. However, the greatest concern during the 1750s was to prevent the offloading of desirable items from East Indiamen (or even naval vessels) as they sailed up the English Channel. Some local ships chased after East Indiamen as far as the Isle of Wight, so instructions were sent to rummage all vessels, and when in 1754 eight ships were   69 expected from St Helena, the Collector was warned: 'take care that eight trusty active and diligent officers be placed on board to prevent any goods from being unshipped'. Vessels of less than 70 tons found to have 100 lb of tobacco or stalks or snuff on board, at anchor or 'hovering' were to be seized.

Things became much worse during the 1760s, when violent gangs were operating. The Beer gang were then landing tea and other goods between Start Point and Torbay, and were sufficiently confident to ride straight through the centre of Exeter. In March 1766 the Collector reported: 'Numerous gangs of desperate men, well mounted, from twenty to forty or fifty and sometimes a hundred are often met in the country and on the Sea Coast. . .' He added that several seizures had been recaptured by the smugglers. Since his officers' lives were frequently in danger, he asked for the assistance of a party of dragoons. This was not forthcoming, but the armed cutter *Friendship* was helping to intercept vessels, and soon brought in one from Torbay, laden with 20cwt of fuller's earth. (This is used in woollen cloth manufacture, and so was an illegal export.) Papers found on another captured vessel gave the names of those illegally exporting wool and fuller's earth from Dartmouth to France. Then the *Laurel*, a naval vessel, seized a cargo of claret on board a ship in Torbay, and another seizure in 1766 included 30 casks of wine and 20 oilskin bags of fine tea, found under a cargo of bricks. The ingenuous captain of a merchant ship tried to bring in a quantity of cocoa from Spain. When this item of personal property was discovered, the captain pleaded first that he had had a bad voyage, and second, that he had been told in San Sebastian that others got away with this, and that 150 bags were on their way to Poole in another vessel. The Dartmouth Collector was unmoved; he judged that ignorance was no defence!

As a typical instance of a seizure, in 1775 the commander of the *Hind* Revenue cutter captured a cutter with tobacco worth over £376, black and green tea valued at £13.16s.10d, spirits worth £170 and 172 pieces of cambric. His share of the prize money for taking a cutter and some £600 worth of cargo must have been encouraging. Among other items seized at this time were figs, nutshells, pepper, coffee and china.

During the fighting against the rebellious American colonies it was essential to prevent arms and gunpowder from
reaching them, and letters and other documents had to be
censored. More and more men were now sent to fight overseas, and the smuggling gangs became bolder and more
violent. In 1775 Henry Mugford, the Waiter and Searcher at
Brixham 'fell over a cliff' and was drowned. Ten years later
Richard Cullin met a similar fate. At sea the struggle inten-
sified. The Revenue cutter *Spider*, based at Dartmouth and
commanded by John Longford patrolled between Portland
and Rame Head, and had Letters of Marque entitling him to
attack French, Spanish or Dutch ships. Three large armed
smuggling vessels were known to be making regular trips
between Guernsey and the south Devon coast at this stage.
The largest was the *Ranger* lugger, built at Cawsand, with 22
guns and a crew of 100, (at over 200 tons she was larger than
any vessel in the Revenue fleet). Her captain was believed to
be the notorious smuggler Wellard. The *Dogger Bank* was the
second large vessel, and the third was the *Swift*, commanded
by William Brown, with 16 guns and a crew of 50. In the early
hours of 13th May 1783 a battle took place which illustrates
the problems faced by the preventive service. The story rum-
bles on for five years in the Collector's correspondence, with
contradictory versions, so that it is difficult to know exactly
what happened. It is mainly reported by John Swaffin, of the
Spider cutter, who on one occasion is called Captain Swaffin,
but he seems to have been in charge of a small boat attached
to the *Spider*, rather than master of the cutter itself. The battle
involved two vessels on each side. Seeking to enforce law and
order were the Revenue cutters *Spider* and *Alarm* (under
Captain Gibbs). The main smuggling vessel was the *Swift*
with her crew of 50, but under her protection was a small
unnamed sloop belonging to Thomas Perkinson of Brixham.
In an equivocal position between these opposing forces was
Mr Prout, the Paignton Customs officer.

John Swaffin maintained that he first saw the *Swift* at
anchor off Paignton, realised she was too powerful for him to
intervene, and so made for the small sloop. He was then seized
by smugglers, taken on board the *Swift* and held prisoner
below decks throughout the ensuing action. (Another version   71

Smugglers' Lane, Holcombe near Teignmouth as shown in a contemporary print. Two smugglers can be seen in the foreground carrying away their casks of illicit spirits while the third rolls his uphill. The lane and beach

beside the Parson and Clerk rocks can still be visited. Reproduced by kind permission of West Country Studies Library, Exeter.

73

implies he swam away and hid!) The *Swift*'s crew then used Swaffin's boat to run their contraband ashore, where a landing party of 100 men was waiting. The cargo was a very valuable one, consisting of 4 tons of tea and 9,000 gallons of spirits. While the unloading was going on, the smugglers brought out Mr Prout from the shore and allowed him to 'seize' Thomas Perkinson's sloop and take her into Brixham as his 'prize'. Swaffin's report continues: 'They landed a considerable quantity on Paignton Sands between the hours of 12 and 4 & would have continued the landing had they not been prevented by my crew and the crew of the *Alarm* . . . who went to the above landing place.' There was an exchange of fire between the *Swift* and the *Alarm* and it was said that the smugglers fully intended to destroy both Revenue vessels, and might have done so had not the battery on Berry Head protected them. Fighting was also taking place on the beach, where John Stanton, a smuggler from Cockington village, was determined to settle old scores. Mistaking William Tizzard (a mariner from Swaffin's boat) for his arch enemy Swaffin, he half murdered him, and would have completed the job had

Cockington Village, Torquay, home of smuggler John Stanton, one of the combatants in the battle in 1783 between the smugglers and the preventive service on Paignton beach.

not Tizzard managed to say who he was. Thomas Pether-bridge, another member of Swaffin's crew, was knocked down by a rock and judged likely to lose an eye. Two more of Swaffin's crew escaped, one by hiding under the boat and the other by swimming away. By 6 am the smugglers decided they could land no more at Paignton, and sailed off (taking Swaffin and his boat with them) and ran the rest of the cargo ashore at Holcombe near Teignmouth. Finally they released Swaffin and his boat. Whatever the exact details, this is a story involving violence and corruption. Moreover, two Revenue cutters backed up by gunfire from the Berry Head battery failed to stop an extremely valuable cargo being brought ashore on Paignton sands that May morning.

Captain Brown and the *Swift* were soon back from Guernsey with more contraband, and threatening the life of Richard Valentine, the Waiter and Searcher at Salcombe (see Chapter 5). The Dartmouth Collector wrote to London: 'we think it almost impossible to convict an offender by a Devonshire Jury who are composed of farmers and generally the greatest part of them either smugglers or always ready to assist them in removing and secreting their goods'. There were brighter moments, however. In October 1790 there was a large seizure of spirits at Dawlish; the smugglers' vessel was captured and several horses, and the crew were sent to serve in the Navy. Two years later the Tide Surveyor at Brixham found on the shore two boxes containing 24 dozen packs of playing cards. All had been repacked in plain paper, and the ace of spades removed. Playing cards were a luxury and subject to heavy duty, indeed until 1960 the ace of spades carried the Excise mark. At Brixham the smugglers were relanding packs on which drawback of duty had been claimed, but one wonders what happened to the holder of the 288 aces! Whoever was responsible subsequently sent a threatening letter to the Brixham Tide Surveyor. Another unexpected development at Brixham concerned the theft of a sloop called *Martin*. Six men had been overheard talking and were judged to be planning piracy!

The war with France ground on, and in July 1800 a Mediterranean fleet of 27 ships under a strong naval escort anchored in Torbay. There were the usual strict instructions

75

to keep a close watch on them to prevent offloading of goods. Two years later the Revenue cutter *Industry*, commanded by John Radcliff was stationed at Dartmouth. She was conspicuously successful, and in a five month period in 1803 captured no fewer than five smuggling vessels. (Her run of good fortune followed an embarrassing episode when the commander went ashore to buy bread at 7 am and was left behind when *Industry* was taken out without authorisation by the Chief Mate.) The same year a naval gunship captured three more smuggling vessels and their cargoes. Losses at this level were forcing a change of tactics; the free traders now sought less defended beaches or sank their tubs offshore for recovery later. This trend was reinforced when the Coast Guard was established in 1822, but small scale seizures continued, and 30 kegs were captured on Dawlish beach that year. Local tradition has preserved several stories which probably date from this time. The Rev S Baring-Gould wrote about 'Sir Thomas ... in his stately home near Dartmouth' whose house was carefully but respectfully searched. The spirits were in the family coach and escaped detection! Another story concerns 'Resurrection' Jackman of Brixham. When the local preventiveman traced a cargo to Jackman's home, he heard wailing in the house. He was told that Jackman was dead and would be buried at Totnes the following night. Accordingly, two men were sent to watch the funeral cortège but were terrified by the sight of a cadaverous Jackman bringing up the rear. Of course the brandy in the coffin reached Totnes safely. (This story, with variations, is also told about Bob Elliot of Brixham and occurs in many other smuggling areas.) Another story concerns a landing at St Mary's Bay, just south of Berry Head. The look-out man who should have drawn off the Coastguard by creating a diversion had overslept, but then raced to the cliffs and acted as a ghost in his flapping night shirt and with his head masked in a dark gansey!

A more prosaic account of events in the 1830s came from an informer at Roscoff, who sent details of a number of small vessels, mainly between 20 and 30 tons, which brought cargoes of 100 to 120 tubs of spirits. The *Louisa*, whose master was known as French Jack, and had recently been released from Bodmin Gaol, was fairly typical. She sometimes made three round trips within a month, and brought brandy (no doubt to order) to Dartmouth, Plymouth or Teignmouth.

There is a rather surprising postscript to this account of smuggling in Torbay. In 1833 naval officers on board HMS *Admiral Hood* were seen sinking tubs off the Kent coast at North Foreland. In the court case which followed, Sir William Courtenay of Powderham Castle near Exeter perjured himself in an attempt to defend his naval colleagues. He was convicted and sentenced to transportation!

PLACES TO VISIT

Smuggler's Lane, Holcombe
This is accessible either by walking north from Teignmouth along the coast path (the seawall beside the railway) to just south of the railway tunnel beside Parson and Clerk rocks or by car down the steep narrow lane below Gatehouse Nursing Home on the east side of A379. There is very limited parking, but this is a genuine smuggling beach!

Shaldon and Ness Beach
Use the large Ness carpark above Shaldon off the bend in A379 at grid reference SX 937718. Shaldon village is worth exploring. The narrow lanes are full of character with a mix of thatched cottages and elegant Regency villas. Ness House, now a hotel, was built by Lord Clifford as a summer family residence in 1810. Immediately behind is the so-called Smugglers' Tunnel down to Ness Beach. A ruined limekiln at the entrance suggests the reason it was cut. The original tunnel led straight down to the beach; there is now a change of direction where a new lit tunnel has been cut, and a further old blocked tunnel can be seen behind the beach. Take a torch! Ness Beach can also be reached from Shaldon along the shore at low tide.

Coombe Cellars Inn
The present buildings are Victorian but on the original site. Approach from Shaldon or Newton Abbot along the minor road, turning north down the steep narrow lane to a large

77

carpark and yacht marina. The ruined jetty is a reminder of times past! The estuary could be forded at this point.

Cockington Village and Torre Abbey, Torquay
Most of Torbay has changed out of all recognition since the smuggling period, but the thatched cottages of Cockington village give some idea of a village where smugglers lived, though the Drum Inn was built by Sir Edwin Lutyens in 1934. St Marychurch has changed drastically since the days when contraband was stored here.

Brixham
Congested but worth exploring, Brixham is a working fishing port with an old harbour and a replica of the *Golden Hind*. Brixham Museum (open main season) incorporates the National Coastguard Museum and has a section on smuggling. Berry Head Country park, well signed from Brixham, is an excellent view point with interesting fortifications both prehistoric and Napoleonic.

The busy harbour at Brixham today, with the replica of The Golden Hind moored in the foreground. The smugglers Resurrection Jackman, Bob Elliot and others operated from Brixham.

Baynard's Wharf, Dartmouth, the quay from which the Pilgrim Fathers sailed. The Old Custom House is the 18th century building on the right.

Dartmouth

Dartmouth is beautifully sited and full of interest. (Central carpark.) The following are well worth a visit: the famous Butterwalk (1635–40) with granite pillars and half timbering; merchant's house of 1763 in Mansion House Street; Dartmouth Castle, 1481; St Petrock's Church, 1763; Old Custom House, 1739, behind the cobbled quay (used in the BBC TV series *Onedin Line*); Baynard's Cove artillery fort of 1537 and the inscription recording the departure of the *Mayflower*; Newcomen's Steam Engine housed adjoining the carpark. The Museum is open weekdays throughout the year. Two ferries cross to Kingswear and boat trips are available up to Totnes and into Torbay.

5
Plymouth Sound and the South Devon Coast

The story of smuggling in south-west Devon is dominated by what happened in and around Plymouth Sound. There are few authentic accounts of episodes before the 1770s, partly because official records have not survived, but also, I suspect, because these coasts remained virtually unwatched up to that time. Outside Plymouth itself there were no more than a handful of Customs officers based at Salcombe, Bantham and Oreston in Devon, and Saltash, St Germans and Cawsand in the bordering areas of Cornwall. Almost all recorded seizures took place at sea, so we can only surmise where the smugglers intended to land their cargoes, nor are there newspaper accounts of what took place before 1799, when the celebrated *Lottery* story began. The limited evidence available suggests that in the 1770s the smugglers were operating particularly in the Salcombe, Hope Cove and Bigbury Bay areas. Thereafter nearly all the action was concentrated between the Yealm estuary on the east, and Cawsand to the west.

The whole coastline between Start Point and the eastern outskirts of Plymouth is exposed and for the most part rocky. A rampart of spectacular cliffs extends between Start Point and Bolt Tail along the most southerly section of the coast. Tough metamorphic rocks sparkle with flakes of mica and crystals of quartz, and create the coves and headlands which are a delight for walkers today, but have long proved a graveyard for shipping. At the heart of this forbidding coast another drowned river valley leads inland to Kingsbridge, past the delightful small port of Salcombe. Though there is a bar at the mouth of this estuary, it offered obvious opportunities for an unobtrusive landing. The best sandy beaches lie further west; Hope Cove was one smuggling beach, and a cave in Bolberry Down above is still called Ralph's Hole after a local smuggler. Burgh Island, a tidal islet off Bigbury, was used by Tom Crocker, a 16th century smuggler, who stored goods in a cave on the island. The Pilchard Inn, once a 14th century pilgrim inn, used to have a carving of Tom on the fireplace, but this has been defaced. Cargoes were run on the sandy beaches of Thurlestone and Challaborough, and there are three long narrow estuaries here where goods were brought in: the Avon (pronounced Awm), the Erme and the Yealm (pronounced Yam). It is this last which the smugglers particularly favoured. In the 1820s and 1830s rafts of tubs which had been sunk offshore were either towed in or carried in by small boats. The Mew Stone at the entrance to Wembury Bay was a hazard to shipping. According to the Rev Baring-Gould, this small island was inhabited by Black Joan and her brother Fyn, the children of an outlaw, who relayed signals to the smugglers. They subsequently moved to another tiny island off Looe. Even today much of the south-west Devon coast is difficult to reach by land. Two centuries ago both the coast and the farming hinterland, the area known as the South Hams, must have been extremely remote.

Burgh Island from the beach at Bantham. The 16th century smuggler, Tom Crocker, lived there and stored his contraband in a cave on the island.

81

The maze of navigable waterways which open into Plymouth Sound has always dominated maritime activity in west Devon or east Cornwall. Plymouth started as a Saxon settlement beside Sutton Pool, but Plympton at the mouth of the river Plym was originally the more important port. Plympton was a stannary town, shipping out tin from Dartmoor, but silt from the tin streaming choked the Plym estuary and the centre of activity shifted to Plymouth itself. What remains of old Plymouth today is the Barbican area and the Quay beside Sutton Pool. Both the Tudor Custom House and its 19th century replacement still stand here, close to the Mayflower Steps, from which the pilgrims sailed. Sutton Pool opens into Cattewater (the Plym estuary) which figures in various smuggling episodes. At Oreston on its further shore a Customs officer was based who frequently received urgent orders to watch for clandestine landings or transshipment of goods. The naval dockyard was begun in 1691 on virgin land to the west, facing the Tamar estuary, here known as Hamoaze. The new town of Dock, as it was called, grew very rapidly because of the importance of the naval base during the Napoleonic Wars. By 1824 it had outstripped Plymouth in population, and was renamed Devonport. Between the dockyard and Plymouth the third settlement of Stonehouse also grew rapidly, and was another destination for smuggled goods. The whole region, including Saltash and Torpoint on the Cornish side of Hamoaze provided the major market for contraband at least until 1850.

Plymouth Sound is a magnificent natural harbour, but sailing vessels could easily be trapped within its sheltered waters by a southerly wind. It is said that when the Armada was sighted, Francis Drake continued his game of bowls precisely because he knew his fleet could not sail out of harbour. The same problem beset naval ships during the Napoleonic Wars, with the result that battleships anchored outside the Sound in Cawsand Bay to the west, or in Torbay. This was one of the factors which made Cawsand in Cornwall the smuggling capital of the whole region. Cawsand (sometimes written Cossan) and its close neighbour Kingsand, then in Devon, grew up in the lee of Rame Head and Penlee Point. When the Duchy of Cornwall imposed heavy dues on the pilchard fishermen operating from Sutton Pool to pay for fortifications on the Hoe, the whole industry moved to Cawsand. With fishing, and the establishment of huge pilchard 'palaces', came shipbuilding, and the skills which were later to create vessels far superior to any in the Revenue service. During the long years of war with France, Kingsand and Cawsand became the supply bases for naval vessels anchored offshore. Lord Nelson and Lady Hamilton used to stay at the Ship Inn! In exactly the same way as Deal in Kent became the supply base for vessels anchored in The Downs and a notorious smuggling centre, so Cawsand and Kingsand prospered. Local men built and manned the smuggling vessels which dominated the industry for many years. It was the building of the mile-long breakwater at the entrance to Plymouth Sound which altered the situation. This huge undertaking was begun by Rennie in 1812, but not completed until 1841. Though smuggling on a more discreet scale continued at least until 1850, the dominant role of Cawsand was at an end.

Returning now to the detail of what took place in the 1770s in the Salcombe area. Something was obviously going on in 1776 when the Dartmouth Collector reported problems there arising from any anonymous letter. Another letter, to the Sheriff of Devon, referred to an informer who was only too anxious to co-operate (for a price). It was confidently expected that they would soon hear all about 'the Prawl People'. The villagers of East Prawle, close to Start Point and above Lannacombe Beach, were clearly up to no good. The best account of what was happening came from Richard Valentine, the Customs officer at Salcombe in 1783: '. . . within the neighbourhood of Salcombe, the practice of smuggling has been carried on by people who live in little villages along the coast who are in general poor and assist in unloading the smuggling vessels and bringing the same to the shore where the horses are in readiness to carry off the same. The species of ship employed on this coast are chiefly fishing craft belonging to Torbay who generally land their cargoes on or near the Start or Prawle at which places myself and the rest of the officers under my direction have kept a constant look-out at nights when the wind is fair, and in times past have made considerable seizures, but the smugglers have altered their

83

proceedings which is that they never land any goods before the horses are in readiness on the spot to take the same away, which are seldom less in number than fifty and often times a hundred at a time and every horse has his rider armed with a loaded whip or a brace of pistols in order to despatch the officers if they attempted to make seizure of the goods...' Richard Valentine further declared that he had been threatened with having his brains blown out, and he reported three armed smuggling vessels. The *Ranger*, built at Cawsand and armed with 22 nine-pounder guns, had just landed a cargo close to Rame Head, and the following day anchored in Hope Cove for ballast and provisions. From Richard Valentine's description it is clear this was a particularly large and well armed vessel. The other smuggling craft were the *Dogger Bank*, which had just landed a cargo at Cawsand and the *Swift*. All three had brought goods from Guernsey. Richard Valentine said he could call on two Tidesmen and three extra men but begged for more help: 'if there was about twelve or fourteen of

84   Unloading a cutter. From a line engraving c.1785.

the horse troop stationed at Kingsbridge ... they'd give a good account of themselves'.

It is interesting that he was calling for a land-based force. There were already several Revenue vessels patrolling at sea, but Warren Lisle, who commanded the whole fleet, was sceptical about the loyalty of its officers. He reported to the Prime Minister that on this stretch of coast most of the cargoes of tea and brandy were brought from Roscoff and came over in fine lugsail vessels, but that the Waterguard made few seizures 'and the shore officers are too much their friends to give them trouble'. Trouble there certainly had been in Hope Cove in May 1788. Surgeon William Pearce wrote: 'I certify that I was called to Philip Cuming & Philip Cove at Hope in Bigbury Bay on the 31st of May last in consequence of their having been assaulted by some smugglers, that I found a compound oblique fracture of Philip Cuming's leg & doubt whether he may not be a cripple. Philip Cove received such violent blows on his head as to lay his skull bare in several places besides several other violent blows about his body & arms.'

Five months earlier there had been even worse trouble in Cawsand Bay. Smugglers had shot and killed one of the crew of a naval boat and wounded others. Another naval boat had seized the smuggling vessel responsible, and this turned out to be the *Revenge* from Guernsey, commanded by Harry Carter (the notorious smuggler from Prussia Cove). Carter and ten smugglers escaped, and £300 was offered for information leading to their capture. This episode was reported in the *Exeter Flying Post*, but appears in a decidedly different light in Harry Carter's autobiography!

Throughout the 1790s the struggle between large armed smuggling vessels and the Revenue cutters continued in and around Plymouth Sound, and led to a whole series of seizures. However, it was still possible in 1792 for four large vessels from Guernsey to land cargoes of tea and tobacco near Cawsand without interruption or opposition. Most seizures were taking place near Cawsand, but goods were being run close to Plymouth itself. The local Exciseman discovered that quantities of spirits were being taken to the army camp at Tamerton Foliot (north of Plymouth), but his attempt to prevent this was thwarted when the commanding officer stationed a sentry to protect the goods.

As the commanders of the Revenue vessels became more determined, the smugglers fell back on greater violence. In January 1795 a smuggler fired on a Custom House boat, killing one of its crew. Soon after this there was an exchange of fire in Hamoaze when a Revenue boat surprised an open galley laden with spirits. One of the smugglers was wounded in the groin, which put an end to the contest and the spirits were seized. In March the following year a full-scale battle took place at Torpoint between the crew of the naval cutter *Viper* and a large contingent of townspeople from Dock (Devonport). One naval seaman was killed and two seriously injured. Eight horses laden with spirits were seized but later recaptured by the smugglers. Then in 1798 Humphrey Glynn was murdered, setting in train the so-called *Lottery* story.

On the night of 26th December 1798 a large smuggling cutter was anchored half a mile south-west of Penlee Point near Cawsand. In brilliant moonlight small boats had come alongside to begin the unloading of a valuable cargo (at least 6,000 gallons of spirits as well as tea and tobacco), and several loads had already been taken towards Cawsand. At this point the Cawsand Customs boat, commanded by Ambrose Bowden, came on the scene. Mr Bowden hailed the smugglers, said who he was, and with enormous if foolhardy courage, declared he was coming to seize the unknown vessel. The smugglers shouted back that they would fire, and did so three times, instantly killing boatman Humphrey Glynn. The Revenuemen then returned the fire, and the smuggling vessel cut her cable and put to sea. This violent episode shocked the whole Customs establishment. At a time when compensation for death or injury while on duty was minimal (£10 for the loss of a hand or foot, for example), special consideration was given to Glynn's ten year old son, who had a serious speech defect. He wanted to become a tailor, and a school was found for him at St Germans. Meanwhile suspicion had grown that the smuggling vessel was the *Lottery*, built at Cawsand, but registered at Looe, which carried a crew of 18 men. One might have expected that the smugglers would have changed the vessel's name or kept clear of Cawsand until things quietened

Cawsand Village and its tiny beach on Plymouth Sound. Probably the most active of all the West Country smuggling communities, and scene of many violent clashes between the smuggling vessels and the Revenue Cutters.

down, but five months later they were back. This time they were spotted off Start Point by the *Hinde* Revenue cutter, commanded by Captain Bray. The smugglers realised they had been seen, and hastily altered course towards Bolt Head. The *Hinde* gave chase and at 5 am next morning the two ships were becalmed off the Lizard some five miles apart. Captain Bray then sent two armed rowboats from the *Hinde* under the mate, Hugh Pearce, to intercept the vessel. The smugglers had covered up the incriminating name *Lottery* and warned that they would open fire if approached. Mindful of the earlier murder, Hugh Pearce and his men withdrew. Then a breeze sprang up and the chase began in earnest. Captain Bray was an able and determined seaman, and the *Hinde* began to overhaul the *Lottery*. The smugglers jettisoned some of their cargo and even tried to row their vessel in a desperate attempt to escape, but by early afternoon, when they were off the Longships light, the *Hinde* was near enough to fire on her adversary. Twelve of the smugglers then jumped into their

87

small boat and rowed for the shore. Two boats from the *Hinde* followed and captured them. The *Hinde* itself then captured the *Lottery* with its cargo and the remaining crew, and Captain Bray sailed into Plymouth in triumph with his prize. The story does not end there. Captain Bray interrogated his prisoners until one man – Roger Toms – talked, and named Thomas Potter as the man who had shot Humphrey Glynn. It was, of course, an unspeakable sin for one smuggler to betray another, and Roger Toms was in mortal danger. As a key witness he had to be kept on board the *Hinde* until all the *Lottery* crew could be brought to justice. But somehow he was enticed ashore and hidden from the authorities. He was taken to the Channel Islands and was about to be shipped to America when his presence was discovered. In April 1800 he was brought back to Exeter under military guard, and ultimately went on to testify at the trial of his crewmates in London.

Once Roger Toms had named Thomas Potter as Glynn's murderer, a troop of Dragoons was sent to seize him at his home in Polperro. (It is not clear why he was not already under lock and key.) The dragoons arrived at midnight and caught Thomas Potter in bed. He was taken to London under armed guard, and was finally convicted and executed just two years after he fired the fatal shot. At the same time 14 other smugglers from Salcombe were taken for trial in London, accused of firing on a Customs boat. The *Lottery* itself had already been judged suitable to join the Revenue fleet. As a temporary Revenue Cutter she was based at Dartmouth, and went on to capture other smuggling vessels.

According to Henry Shore, Roger Mark had been another member of the *Lottery* crew who seems to have slipped through the net and gone back to smuggling. In January 1802 he was the helmsman of a boat which very nearly escaped from a pursuing Revenue vessel, but was shot and died at sea at the age of 40. He is buried at Talland church, near Polperro, where his memorial stone can still be seen:

'In the prime of life most suddenly,
Sad tidings to relate
Here view my utter destiny,

And pity my sad state.
I by a shot which rapid flew
Was instantly shot dead;
Lord pardon the offender who
My precious blood did shed.'

It is an appropriate epitaph to the whole *Lottery* story.

These were war years when trading vessels in the Channel ran the gauntlet of armed privateers from several nations. In 1797, for example the *Diamond* from Dundee, returning from Jamaica with sugar, rum and coffee came into Plymouth, having been captured by a French privateer three days earlier, and then retaken off Start Point by a Plymouth lugger. A vessel from Whitehaven carrying invalid soldiers had a similar experience. But despite the warfare, smuggling continued. Indeed, winter storms may still have been the greatest hazard. In January 1793 the Guernsey vessel *Maria* was caught in a fearful storm off Rame Head. Three crewmen were washed overboard. Three other men and the master (who owned both the vessel and cargo) managed to hold onto the mainsail. To save their lives they sailed into Cattewater, Plymouth, carrying their cargo of 204 ankers of brandy and other goods. An unsympathetic Customs officer took all their possessions, including part of their clothing!

At this stage the Plymouth Customs compiled a list of 16 vessels thought to be making as many as ten trips a year and bringing in around 70,000 gallons of spirit annually to the Plymouth area. In a five week period in the summer of 1799, for example, the officers and boatmen captured 855 gallons of brandy and gin, mainly near Cawsand and Oreston, but none was taken by the Riding Officers at Saltash, Calstock or Sheviock, or the boats based in the Erme and Yealm rivers. The flood of cheap illicit liquor was often distributed locally by the women of Cawsand, who staggered in bloated fashion, with bladders concealed among their clothing. No wonder the Mayor, Aldermen and merchants of Saltash begged for additional Revenue vessels to patrol Plymouth Sound, because of the damage done to legitimate traders. Local merchants were regularly allowed to buy seized spirits for resale, but there were frequent crises over the lack of secure storage.

89

When the *Britannia* was seized in June 1800, two warehouses had to be hired (at £1.1.0d a week) to store the 1,000 casks of spirits and a quantity of tobacco she had been carrying. Four years later, when the Customs House was holding 15,000 gallons of contraband spirit in 2,500 casks, some made with very thin staves, there was more trouble! Yet another, slightly cheaper warehouse had to be hired a few months later for 764 casks and 20 bags of tobacco from another capture. Not surprisingly the Collector suggested that seized spirits should, after treatment, go to the Navy rather than be sold locally or destroyed. It was also inevitable that the storehouses were robbed; three warehouses were broken into on 19th April 1809 alone.

Devon cider was a source of trouble to the local Exciseman. If offered for sale it was liable to duty, and in default of payment could be seized. Mr Balkwill, a farmer living near Kingsbridge, sought to reclaim 80 hogsheads (4,200 gallons)

Smugglers' wives frequently feigned pregnancy, carrying dutiable goods concealed under their clothing. This contemporary print shows Lovey Warne of Hampshire transporting silk fabrics, while the women of Cawsand were swathed in bladders filled with spirits.

of cider 'for private consumption' and after a year's struggle and the intervention of two local gentlemen, not only did he get his own 80 hogsheads, but a further 107 belonging to other farmers were released. So in 1818 the farmers round Kingsbridge celebrated in style as almost 10 thousand gallons of cider were returned, and all (of course!) for private consumption. A shipwright from Salcombe rigged and decorated a boat on wheels to carry cider casks at the head of a procession of 45 wagons and carts, all escorted by the local cavalry. There was dancing in the streets, a large sheep was roasted and a mere 157½ gallons of cider consumed!

At sea smuggling continued unabated, in fact the volume probably increased after the end of the Napoleonic Wars, though the techniques had changed. The larger vessels had now been abandoned in favour of small half-decked ones, carrying 400 or 500 gallons of spirit each (tobacco and salt were other cargoes). Open galleys employed in seine netting also took part, and under cover of their normal activities, grappled up tubs which had been sunk offshore. The Eddystone Lighthouse (Smeaton's tower, which now stands on Plymouth Hoe) was a recognised marker when sinking the rafts of tubs. Henry Shore, who had good reason to know what had happened, declared that smuggling reached a peak here between 1825 and 1835, when tobacco had become a very profitable cargo. He compiled a list of 52 boats and 81 men from Cawsand who made at least occasional trips to Roscoff, and some shuttled back and forth repeatedly, even making two deliveries from France within a week. Passenger vessels also took part, and the individual passengers seized their opportunities. One man was caught at Stonehouse in 1817 with a bedstead full of lace.

Bad weather continued to take its toll. The well-known smuggling vessel belonging to Philip Kingcup was wrecked on the Mewstone in a storm. All hands were lost and the empty hulk was driven onshore in Hope Cove, with all the tubs hung round her, ready for sinking. (Philip Kingcup's brother Richard was another smuggler, but a third brother was a naval Admiral.) In March 1834 another smuggling vessel was wrecked on the unfinished Plymouth breakwater, while being chased by a Revenue cutter at 1 am. The crew saved them-

Hope Cove, South Devon, where Phillip Kingcup's smuggling vessel was washed ashore with all hands lost.

selves by clinging to the cranes and were rescued next morning by a light vessel.

Twenty-two years after the Coastguard was established, and when there were no fewer than 75 shore-based men operating in the Plymouth area, smuggling still went on. Some seizures were in relatively isolated areas, at Challaborough in Bigbury Bay or near Salcombe, for example, but others took place within Plymouth Sound. In December 1837 the *Louise* of Dartmouth was spotted by the Coastguards at Cremyl, who gave chase. The *Louise* ran before the wind to the jetty at Stonehouse, where the crew escaped, leaving the vessel and her cargo of 140 bales of tobacco as well as spirits. Two years later another sloop was boarded in Cattewater and found to contain 3,000 lb of manufactured tobacco and six bales of tobacco stems, a cargo liable to a duty of £1,500. The master and mate pleaded guilty and went to prison. What finally killed the free trade here was not the preventive services, but the cuts in duty which rendered smuggling unprofitable.

PLACES TO VISIT

The South Devon coast between Start Point and the outskirts of Plymouth is remarkably undeveloped and often hard to reach down desperately narrow roads. It includes some magnificent stretches of the South West Coast Path, notably between Start and Prawle Points and from Bolt Head to Bolt Tail. Another recommended walk is round the carriage drive built early this century for Lord Revelstoke, just south of the river Yealm, round Gara Point in Wembury Bay. Warren Point National Trust carpark at grid reference SX 541466, south of Noss Mayo, is a convenient starting point.

Salcombe
Beware steep hills and double yellow lines! (Carpark on southern edge.) Salcombe is congested but most attractive. The Custom House, with a fine crest and pink-washed walls stands on the quay, with its balcony overlooking the harbour. The Maritime and Local History Museum, open daily main season, has a photographic record of US troops training for the Normandy Landings in the Second World War. There is a ferry to East Portlemouth and pleasure trips up the estuary to Kingsbridge in the main season.

Inner Hope Cove and Bolt Tail
The smuggling beach at Inner Hope is very obvious. The old village centre with authentic thatched cottages is set back from the coast in a sheltered hollow below the Coastguard cottages. Walk up the signed coast path onto Bolt Tail for an excellent view right round Bigbury Bay. There is an alternative view point on Bolberry Down; the carpark here is at SX 689385, approached from Bolberry village. The footpath to Soar Mill Cove is worth exploring.

Bantham, Bigbury and Burgh Island
The Pilchard Inn on Burgh Island is the most popular attraction. (Carpark at Bigbury-on-Sea.) Walk across the sands at low tide, or travel on the remarkable tracked vehicle at high tide. Bantham is still unspoilt. (Carpark at SX 663437 among

93

sand dunes beside Avon Estuary.) A passenger ferry sometimes runs across, but check the times.

Cawsand and Kingsand

Take the direct passenger ferry in high season from Plymouth,
or regular passenger ferry from Admiral's Hard, Plymouth to
Cremyll, and walk round the coast through the delightful
grounds of Mount Edgcumbe (3½ miles). If arriving by car,
use the free carpark behind Cawsand. The beach, between
green and purple slate cliffs, seems very small considering
what went on here! Solid stone houses line the waterfront. The
Smugglers' Inn dominates the small square; further on is the
Old Ship Inn where Nelson stayed with Lady Hamilton. Pass
the former county boundary to enter Kingsand, above another
small beach with views of Plymouth Sound and the breakwater. The coast path south from Cawsand on the way to
Penlee Point and Rame Head passes Pier Cellars, a pilchard
palace where oil was pressed from the stacked fish.

6
Fowey and
the Fishing Villages
of East Cornwall

Rame Head was not so much a boundary between smuggling territories, as a magnificent lookout point and signalling station, with Cawsand to the east and the long sandy beaches of Whitsand (or Whitesand) Bay to westward. St Michael's Chapel on its summit is ancient, though much rebuilt, and was for long a beacon and seamark. Anyone who takes a car to the parking place beyond Rame church will appreciate the position and understand what happened at 3 am on 9th March 1828. Three preventivemen had hidden themselves among gorse bushes in a field some 300 yards from Rame Head. Below them to the west in Polhawn Cove a landing party waited, and a vessel was coming in to run a cargo. Someone spotted the preventivemen, and a fire was immediately lit to warn off the landing. Three men ran into the field carrying blazing straw and reeds, to make more signals. The preventivemen gave chase, but various smugglers escaped. In the end two, John Brown and John Dunstan, were found guilty, and William Borlase not guilty of 'making fires on the sea coast'. John Dunstan's brother Joseph was apparently not charged, though certainly on the scene. (The two Dunstans were dedicated free traders whose names recur in all contemporary reports.) Above Cawsand Bay, Maker church offered other facilities. On one occasion when the local vicar took the Rural Dean up the tower to admire the view, they saw 23 tubs of spirit stacked in a gutter on the roof between the aisle and the nave!

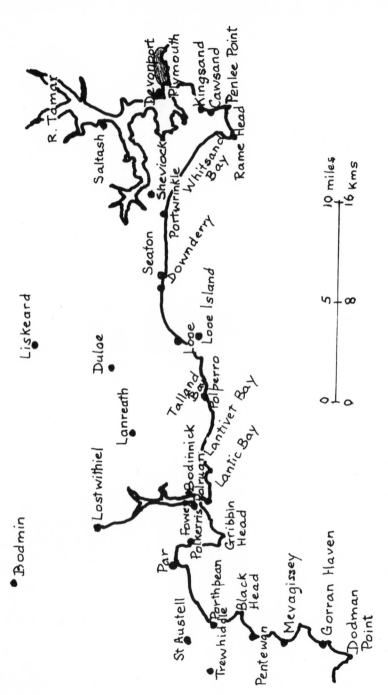

Places associated with the smuggling trade in east Cornwall.

The view westward from Rame Head takes in the whole sweep of coast as far as Dodman Point, and embraces a series of fishing villages and small ports, once the home of smuggling communities, and now favourite holiday resorts. The sea has cut into the folded and contorted beds of slate, grey at Rame Head, but often green or purple, leaving beaches among jagged rocks and backed by steep slopes rising to some 300 or 400 ft. As its name implies, Whitsand Bay has a four mile sweep of sand, but elsewhere there are only small pockets of sand and sheltered coves convenient for a landing. The one exception is the magnificent drowned river valley which opens between Fowey and Polruan, and once carried shipping as far inland as Lostwithiel. Almost all the little ports along this coast had carried on fishing and trading (and often piracy) for centuries before 1700, and smuggling here probably reached a peak between 1780 and 1840, years when there was a ready market for contraband among the mining communities a short distance inland.

The sequence of favoured landing places starts with the sands of Whitsand Bay (the military road and forts on the hills above date from after 1850). In the 1770s a huge cave was hacked out of Sharrow Point by a man claiming it was to cure his gout, but one does wonder! Portwrinkle has only a tiny harbour, yet it took part in pilchard fishing, as the remains of a 15th century pilchard palace show. The records indicate that contraband was carried through Craft Hole and Sheviock beyond. Downderry and Seaton also figure in the story, but the best landing sites were around Looe, from Millendreath Beach and Plaidy in the east, to Hannafore Point and Port Nadler in the west. The twin boroughs at Looe date back nearly 800 years. In 1436 they were joined by a fine bridge (replaced in the 19th century) and particularly in East Looe one can see the evidence of former importance and prosperity in the Guildhall and other older buildings. In the medieval period Looe traded with Bordeaux, exporting tin and fish and importing wine. It also became the port for Liskeard, a town at the heart of mining country. Small boats could carry goods up the river estuary beyond Looe, avoiding the need to use pack animals, and in 1825 a canal was begun which ran up to Moorwater, just west of Liskeard. Dartmoor granite was

97

shipped out this way to build the Thames Embankment and much else. Looe Island added greatly to the attractions of the area from a smuggling point of view. For some years the outlaw's children Black Joan and her brother Fyn lived an unconventional life here, after moving from the Mew Stone. Newspaper reports speak of Jocabed Hooper and his sister Amran; it is not clear whether these are alternative names. The strange pair ate all the rabbits and rats, but they also relayed signals for the smugglers. As on other coasts, a code was agreed whereby a man riding a white horse gave the all clear, but if he passed on foot, the preventives were about. The island became a major depot, and the smugglers were charged a regular fee for storage. One important hiding place came to light when a restless cow kicked a hole through her shed floor into an underlying cave, directly accessible from the sea. Some cargoes were evidently carried towards the mining settlements along the ridgeway route northwards. We know Duloe church was a depot, and it was said that so much spirit was stacked on the more accessible side of the tower that the whole structure was skewed by the weight. Significantly, an Excise officer was murdered at Liskeard, and some spirits were carried as far as Jamaica Inn at Bolventor.

The coast path leading westwards from Looe passes a whole succession of small bays the smugglers regularly used. First comes Talland Bay, with two small coves among slate cliffs. These secluded beaches look exactly as one would expect a smugglers' landing place to be. On the steep hill above stands Talland church, a fine building with carved bench ends and well cut slate gravestones, one of which records the death of Robert Mark, shot at sea in 1802, and probably a crew member of the *Lottery*. Talland Bay has more recent claims to fame. In 1975 a gang known as the Race Horse Set began running drugs from North Africa to Torbay. They later moved operations to a more discreet site at Talland, bringing cannabis on the converted trawler *Guiding Lights*, to be run on shore by rubber dinghy and stored under the floor of the cafe on the hillside above. Their activities were brought to an abrupt end on a moonlit night in September 1979 when 40 members of 'Operation Cyril' watched them bring in 2½ tons of cannabis. The gang's south London headquarters in Penge

The secluded beach at Talland Bay, where the modern day activities of a drug running gang were brought to an abrupt end by 'Operation Cyril' in 1979.

was raided the same night, and ultimately 13 men were convicted at the Old Bailey.

The Talland and Looe smugglers two centuries ago devised various ghost stories to keep prying eyes away. Some are attributed to the Rev Richard Dodge, vicar of Talland between 1713 and 1746. The best known concerns Battling Billy, who transported goods inland by coffin. There are also the usual accounts of women concealing tubs of spirit beneath their skirts, in this case at the Jolly Sailor Inn at West Looe. E S Shapcott recorded that an overgrown lane near Tencreek Farm (½ mile north of Talland church) was still known as Smugglers' Hideyhole Lane in 1928.

A mile beyond Talland Bay is the delightful (but often overcrowded) small port of Polperro. Fishing has been important here for at least 600 years; there were 300 local fishing vessels in 1850, some fishermen still operate today and cellars for fish storage remain. The harbour is partially sheltered by Peak Rock, but was badly damaged in 1774, 1817 and again in 1824. Polperro was the home base for innumerable smug-

99

glers, including members of the *Lottery* crew. It is also celebrated as the home of the smugglers' banker, Zephania Job
(whose story is told later in this chapter).

The coast path next skirts the wide Lantivet Bay, below
Lansallos, and Lantic Bay. Steep slopes back these beaches
and the shores are difficult to reach even today. West Combe
in Lantivet Bay was a favourite landing site, and goods were
hidden in an adit mine belonging to a farmer at Trevarder.
One of the monuments at the fine Lansallos church commemorates another smuggler, employing the same inscription
as at Talland! A cave in Lantic Bay was used during one of the
last major encounters between the smugglers and preventive
forces which took place in 1835. The parson and other residents at Lanreath, on the obvious route inland, were known to
be sympathetic, and the smuggling inn is still there.

Fowey and Polruan are magnificently situated on either
side of the drowned lower valley of the Fowey river. Lostwithiel was the earliest port here and a stannary town entitled
to export tin legally, but silt from the workings blocked the
harbour and Fowey had already taken its place 600 years ago.
It became very important for exporting tin, fish and woollen
cloth and importing French wine, and sent men and ships to
join the king's forces fighting France and Scotland. In the 15th
century its seamen, the Fowey Gallants, engaged in piracy
and brought reprisals from France and Spain. As at Dartmouth, the estuary mouth was fortified and could be closed by
a chain. The present Ship Hotel dates from these stirring
times. It was built by John Rashleigh, a celebrated merchant,
and named after his ship, the *Frances of Fowey* in which he
sailed with his cousins, Drake and Raleigh. The Georgian
Custom House has a large chimney for burning tobacco, and
there are other buildings which the smugglers would recognise. Today Fowey exports china clay rather than tin, and its
economy is built on tourism rather than the free trade, though
it still has a smugglers' festival! In 1824 it had a celebrated
smuggling mayor, and the trade was still going on in 1850.
The shore at Golant, the Bodinnick Ferry, the beaches at
Coombe Hawne and the park at Menabilly (where Daphne du
Maurier later lived) were all involved.

100 The shores of St Austell Bay have been greatly changed as a

Fowey Harbour; a view from the Coastguard cottages at Polruan. Smuggling continued here up until the mid 19th century and is celebrated annually with a smugglers' festival.

result of mineral working, but the tiny port of Polkerris preserves various features from the smuggling years. Polkerris joined in the pilchard fishing, and has the ruins of an Elizabethan pilchard palace and limekilns from its former coastwise trade. A preventive boat was based here in the early 19th century, a sure sign of illicit landings. By contrast the harbour at Par was begun in 1828, originally to export copper ore, but was soon shipping out china clay. Par Sands, white from the clay, are also a recent creation. Charlestown is another artificial harbour, named after Charles Rashleigh, who called in Smeaton to build it at what had been called West Polmeare. The harbour was begun in 1791, again for copper export, and the village behind still keeps its period flavour. Beyond Duporth Holiday Camp are several sandy beaches between Porthpean and Gwendra Point. A Watch House was built at Porthpean in the 1830s, and we know from the reminiscences of a gardener then employed on the Penrice estate that all sorts of illegal happenings took place around Castle Gotha and Lobb's Shop. At Pentewan, the next bay down the coast, 101 the harbour was opened in 1826, and we know that Richard Kingcup was still smuggling here in 1850. A horse tramway linked the port to the mining areas near St Austell, but the harbour became silted up after the last cargo was shipped in the 1930s. The insatiable demands of the local miners ensured a ready market for the spirits landed on all these beaches.

Mevagissey is not only an ancient fishing port but is still operational (despite its popularity with tourists). Its inner harbour dates from the 16th century, and was rebuilt in 1775. At that time Mevagissey was the fourth largest centre of population in Cornwall, and exported 35 million pilchards annually to Italy alone. It also built ships (as Portmellon still does), indeed the smuggling vessels built here were regarded as the very best obtainable. During the Napoleonic Wars it built more ships than any other Cornish town, and after 1815 there was a great expansion of pilchard fishing, necessitating further harbour works. Needless to say Mevagissey also smuggled, and a preventive boat was already based here by 1818.

The last smuggling beach on this stretch of coast was at Gorran Haven, in the shelter of Dodman Point. This is another ancient fishing port, with pilchard cellars and a quay dating from the 16th century. It proved necessary to establish a preventive boat here by 1810; a Watch House was added later, and still stands by the harbour.

This whole length of coast is classic smuggler country, and all the signs are that landings before the 1780s were virtually unopposed. Two instances at Mevagissey show how it was done. In the first, in 1719, the smugglers were caught by that most feared institution, the pressgang. In the second, some 60 years later, they were opposed by determined officers from a Revenue cutter (an infrequent event to judge by contemporary reports of widespread corruption). On both occasions the smuggling vessels were effectively touting for custom in Mevagissey Bay, and enthusiastically received by the local population. There is little doubt that the same thing happened at Fowey and Looe, but we lack details because the official records at Fowey were deliberately destroyed in 1878.

In June 1719 the smack *Mary* under Lieutenant Dilke had come into Fowey in order to impress men for the Navy. The Mayor, perhaps to rid himself of this unpleasant visitor, told

102

Dilke of a strange brigantine which had been seen in Mevagissey bay for several days. This unknown ship was hovering offshore acting as a floating supermarket in effect, and had attracted customers by firing a gun. Little boats from the locality brought eager customers, but no Customs man was allowed on board. The ship was known to be armed. Lieutenant Dilke set off in pursuit of this tempting target, and four hours later caught sight of her. The smuggling vessel tried to escape westward but in the absence of a breeze the pressgang party slowly gained, towing their vessel by rowing their six-oared boat. During this slow motion chase the smuggling crew and all the contraband were ferried ashore in small boats, so that when the pressgang finally reached the brigantine, only the ship's master and two Customs officials were left on board. The ship was flying French colours, and the master claimed to be from Nantes, but later admitted he was Irish. Though the cargo had already been landed, treasonable papers were found on board, and four of the crew were later seized by the pressgang.

On the second occasion, crewmen on the Revenue cutter *Hawke* spotted an unknown vessel off Dodman Point, by the light of an April dawn in 1780. The *Hawke* gave chase, forcing this ship to tack towards Mevagissey. The *Hawke*'s commander, Ambrose Nicholls then realised his quarry was the well-known smuggler *Active*, armed with 18 guns and altogether too strong for him to tackle. He hailed the *Active* saying that he was sending his mate, Hugh Wakeham to inspect her, but the smuggler's master, William Gefford claimed the *Active* was a licensed privateer, and he had no right to examine her. Very sensibly Nicholls decided to seek additional help. He left Hugh Wakeham in charge of a boat's crew to keep an eye on things, and then sailed off to Fowey. With the Collector of Customs, he sought help from the commanding officer of the military forces stationed at Fowey, and was able to embark two officers and 22 privates. With these reinforcements the *Hawke* hoisted her colours and set off back in pursuit of the *Active*. Meanwhile the smugglers had fired on, and done their best to run down Wakeham and his boatcrew, while also offloading their cargo into small boats from Mevagissey. The boatcrew were forced ashore at Vault (or Bow) Sand, just east

103

The busy fishing port of Mevagissey where secret passages and tunnels leading back from the waterfront could still be found as late as 1930.

of Dodman Point, where Wakeham and the local Customs officer climbed up the cliffs and saw that the *Active* was already sailing away up Channel. Determined not to be left empty handed, Wakeham's men then chased one of the small Mevagissey boats, forced the four men inside to jettison some of their brandy kegs, and managed to recognise one of the four as Bovey Dunstone, a Mevagissey fisherman. He, of course, indignantly claimed to have bought the brandy fairly. The final encounter between the *Hawke* and the *Active* took place that afternoon. The *Hawke* fired a gun to force the *Active* to heave to, but in return she fired three guns point blank back. The smugglers must then have realised that the *Hawke* was carrying soldiers, and they surrendered. A crew of 29 was found on board (the master had escaped ashore in Mevagissey); most of the cargo had already been landed but there was still some gin, tea and 57 pieces of china on the ship.

Mevagissey itself was well supplied with hiding places. According to the *Western Morning News* of 19th March 1930, a subterranean passage once led back 70 or 80 yards from the

harbour to the Old Post Office and Mr Roberts' shop opposite. The latter had a stone inscribed 'J.J.D. 1791' on the front
wall. Inside there was a trapdoor to the cellar and a stairway
through the cob wall to the eaves. Entrance to the eaves could
also be gained by pulling out the bottom drawer of a ward-
robe. The Old Post Office had a similar secret chamber, and
many other houses, built over fish cellars, had other possible
concealments.

The years of warfare with France between 1793 and 1815
mark the period when armed smuggling vessels gradually lost
ground in the face of more determined and better equipped
Revenue cutters. Press reports chart frequent captures; a new
sloop at Mevagissey in 1792, for example, a number from
Fowey, and one from Polperro in 1803. Yet at the same time it
was said that the *Unity* made 500 trips before being caught in
Hamoaze in 1800, with a large quantity of spirits and tobacco
on board. (Because the same name was often used when a
vessel was replaced, one can seldom be sure whether this is the
same ship or merely her namesake.)

Polperro was particularly involved in the free trade at this
time, and it may have been because local men were implicated
in the murder of Humphrey Glynn that the first preventive
boat in the country was stationed at Polperro in 1801. Zephania Job's activities in Polperro are particularly intriguing. He
taught at the local school, and the smugglers were keen that
their children should be able to keep records and manage the
conversion of £s to francs, or vice versa. Zephania Job then
acted as smugglers' book-keeper himself, and became the
agent who paid the Guernsey merchants. He charged 1% plus
postage, and is said to have sent abroad some £6,000 a year!
He went on to own a bank in Polperro, and even issued his
own notes. When he died in 1822, payment was temporarily
suspended, until it was clear that he had been a very rich man
(owning quays, limekilns, shares in fishing vessels, and so on)
so no creditor suffered! Indeed his activities are said to have
brought prosperity to the town.

At this stage new mines were being developed near St
Austell, including Fowey Consols at Tywardreath, Crinnis at
Carlyon bay and one at Polgooth. Probably as a result the
beaches at Porthpean were particularly popular for landings. 105

The old Watch House at Polperro, well placed to oversee activities in the harbour.

In 1819, 200 casks were seized on these shores, part of a cargo landed by a Dutch vessel. The remaining 150 casks were spirited away by methods we can understand, thanks to the memories of Mr Hewett, a gardener at Penrice. (His recollections are preserved in Cornwall County Record Office). He was living in the old thatched Manor House in 1836, but remembered how goods were brought from La Rochelle on the Bay of Biscay. A smuggling vessel could remain in shelter at St Martin on the Isle de Ré until there was a favourable wind. Then it was 'up to Ushant' off the western tip of Brittany, and so to Porthpean, The Bite or Hallane (on Black Head). There were two caves in the cliffs, one at high tide mark near Lower Silvermine (due east of Castle Gotha) and another with a square hole, accessible to boats, at Lower Porthpean (which Mr Hewett called Conjuie Beach). The goods were carried on mule or donkey back up the gully to Lobb's Shop, from where a tunnel was said to lead to Penrice House. Other precautions to trap the preventivemen included secret passageways to two cottages, trapdoors into the cellar and a water-filled shaft.

FOWEY AND THE FISHING VILLAGES OF EAST CORNWALL

According to Mr Hewett, the last smuggling run here was made by the *Saucy Joe* in September 1836. The vessel was beached near Gwendra Point at half tide and successfully unloaded. All those with shares in the venture were then informed, and one old salt arrived with a bag of gold guineas. The preventivemen had been 'well grogged' and were safely installed in the 'big house'. There was already a Watch House at Porthpean at this time, as well as Riding Officers at Pentewan and Polgooth. The records indicated that landings had been made on Porthpean beaches for at least 60 years: there are references to an 18th century ship's account book and ledgerbooks for customers and debtors. Canon Mitchell, Vicar of St Austell, appeared several times among the debtors! One of the distribution points inland was named as Becky's Turning, in St Mewan parish, west of St Austell, and there are references to the carriage of goods through Ruddlemoor towards Bodmin, on what is now A391.

The economy of Fowey was equally geared to the free trade. Smuggling vessels from Fowey carried contraband throughout south-west England; in addition other ships brought goods to be run within the port, and the most famous instance of this occurred on 24th July 1824. The cutter *L'Union* of Brest was in the habit of coming into Fowey once a month in ballast, before taking English goods back to France. On this particular voyage french silks, brandy and wine were found on board when *L'Union* was searched by Customs men. The captain, who was a friend of John Bennet, the Mayor of Fowey, may have dropped hints about who knew of his regular 'ballast', and two days later both men were summoned to the Custom House. Officials then followed the Mayor to his home and demanded admission. Initially this was refused, but when the Collector arrived, the door was opened. Quantities of wine and several casks of brandy were found. From overhead came the sound of breaking bottles, and after forcing their way into an upstairs room, the officers found the Mayor busily breaking bottles of wine and brandy, and the floor three inches deep in alcohol! Much of this flowed out into the river, but what remained was said to be worth £300. Incredibly, a month after this disgraceful episode, the Mayor was appointed Lloyd's agent at Fowey!

Labouring men also had their consolations around Fowey. In April 1825 tubs of spirit were washed ashore between Fowey and Polperro (no doubt part of a sunken raft dislodged by a storm). A Polperro man fishing at Cannis Rock, off Gribbin head, hauled in about 40 and was well rewarded when he took these to Fowey Custom House. But the miners of Wheal Howell (east of Fowey) managed to conceal their finds underground and drank themselves into such a state that they could hardly be brought to the surface. Cases of alcoholic poisoning were not uncommon elsewhere, for example a man-servant at Morval near Looe died through drinking to excess in 1817. One can perhaps sympathise with a farmer from Downderry who was found dead drunk in a hedge at Craft Hole in 1833, after his vessel *Dove* had been caught by Cawsand preventivemen in July, and by the Looe Coastguard in August, with the loss in total of 157 tubs! The local Coastguards were not always as successful as their numbers would suggest (in 1844 there were 78 men in the Fowey district in addition to 21 on board the *Fox* Revenue vessel). But then two Fowey Coastguards and one from Polruan had to be dismissed in 1833 on suspicion of smuggling. Moreover, Richard Kingcup, who was a Fowey Coastguard from 1824 to 1828, went on to run the Crown & Anchor Inn on the Quay, while continuing to smuggle at least until 1850. He had mixed fortunes, for example when his men sank 108 tubs off the Dodman, they only retrieved 40 because of the rocks, and on another occasion he was caught on a new schooner in Par Harbour, but he persevered!

The last significant run employing old style techniques took place in Lantic Bay, east of Polruan in March 1835. The smugglers failed because their communications network was defective. The *Daniel & William*, ostensibly a passenger boat, but also regularly employed in the free trade, landed a cargo at Lantic Bay, but as no tubmen had arrived to carry this up the very steep slopes behind the beach, the casks were temporarily hidden in a cave. Early next morning the Revenue vessel *Fox* passed the beach going westwards and one of the smugglers established that she was on her way to Falmouth, and would give them no further trouble. So the laborious business of fetching the tubs and carrying them up some 350 ft began.

About 100 men took part, evidently because many could only manage one tub in addition to the sticks and clubs they held. As it happened two Coastguards from Polruan were sitting smoking behind a hedge above the bay, and overheard one of the passing tubmen remark that the weather was so bad that no Coastguards would be about that night. Coastguard Walter Harper went quietly off to get help, while Coastguard Stevens remained hidden in gorse bushes near Pencarrow Point, watching the party descend to pick up the brandy. Presently Harper and four other guards returned and Stevens fired to show where he was. The six then attempted to capture some of the tubmen. A violent struggle took place in which Stevens was knocked unconscious, but five men were captured. Meanwhile the Revenue cutter *Fox* had completed her business in Falmouth and returned unexpectedly early to

The chase and battle at sea.

Fowey. On hearing of the landing in Lantic Bay, her commander immediately sent a party there on foot. In the end 484
gallons of brandy were seized and the five captured tubmen
were sent for trial (the others presumably escaped). The
prisoners were charged with 'assisting others in landing and
carrying away prohibited goods, some being armed with
offensive weapons'. The jury found them not guilty, a reflec-
tion of public attitudes still prevailing in 1835! As a result of
this episode, a Watch House was built in neighbouring Lantivet Bay, where it can still be seen.

Ten years later there was a landing at Coombe Hawne, a
mile south-west of Fowey. The authorities had been alerted by
an Exciseman at Lostwithiel who noticed two covered wagons
outside a public house. He managed to catch a glimpse of
creep lines inside and immediately informed the preventive
services at Fowey. It was a terrible night, with thunder and
sheets of rain. The boatmen patrolling the harbour entrance
saw a flash of light but took this for lightning. In fact the
smugglers had used the Bodinnick ferryboat to creep up their
tubs. The landing party was waiting in Coombe Hawne cove,
and there was a wagon parked near Menabilly Lodge, just off
Coombe Lane. At this point Coastguard Piper went down into
the bay on the lookout. He was promptly seized and tied up,
but just managed to fire his pistol, giving the warning flash the
boatmen had seen. The smugglers now realised their activities
were discovered; rather surprisingly they disappeared, aban-
doning about 400 gallons of overproof brandy on the beach
beside the Bodinnick ferryboat, swamped by the swell.

PLACES TO VISIT
A popular stretch of coast, with interesting but often crowded
fishing villages.

East and West Looe
East Looe, with its quays, shipping and fishmarket, cluster of
old buildings and sandy beach has most to offer. Granite from
Dartmoor is much in evidence. See the tiny 16th century
Guildhall with porch and outer stair, now a museum (open
main season daily except Saturday) for displays of local

history and smuggling. The Cornish Museum, in a former fish cellar, (open daily main season) has displays of local crafts. A Smugglers' Restaurant boasts an authentic tunnel. There are boat trips along the coast and round Looe Island in main season.

Talland Bay and Church

Walk round the Coast Path from West Looe or Polperro, or by car down steep and narrow lanes to the carpark close to the beach. There are two small bays between cliffs of slate. The sandy beach in the western bay is the obvious and evocative landing site. The church on the hillside above has fine carved bench ends; Robert Mark's memorial is inside the south-west corner of the church.

Polperro

Delightful out of season! Cars must park well back from the village and coast. There are highly photogenic harbour scenes with stone and colour-washed houses rising in tiers above. Look for the Old Watch House commanding the east side of the inner harbour, and House-on-Props by Roman Bridge (home of historian Jonathan Crouch). The museum of Smuggling in Talland Street (open daily main season) is the best of its kind.

The Coast between Lansallos and Polruan

Lansallos church is very fine, and has the grave of a smuggler killed by a cannon ball near the gate outside. More narrow roads give access to an excellent section of South West Coast Path through land protected by the National Trust. Lansallos Beach (otherwise Lantivet Bay) a crescent of sand between lilac and green slates has signs of wheelmarks! The coast west of here was the scene of a smuggling episode in 1835. The Old Watch House stands on the hillside further west. At Polruan the best view of Fowey is from the carpark signed beyond the Coastguard cottages. There is a passenger ferry to Fowey from Polruan and a car ferry from Bodinnick.

Fowey

In a magnificent hillside setting Fowey and its harbour must   111 be explored on foot. (Various signed carparks; summer park-and-ride bus service.) Fowey has picturesque buildings from five centuries: Ship Inn of 1570, once the town house of John Rashleigh; Georgian Custom House; 18th century Town Hall incorporating part of an earlier prison, now the town museum; 14th century church of St Fimbarrus (partly destroyed in a French raid of 1457); Noah's Ark in Fore Street, a merchant's house and warehouse dating from before the fire of 1457, and Place House, a 13th century mansion above the church, largely rebuilt in Regency Gothic, home of the Teffry family. An excellent coast walk to the south-west passes St Catherine's Point and Castle and the smuggling beaches of Readymoney Cove and Polridmouth to Gribbin Head. Check the dates of various festivals and regattas.

Lower Porthpean Beach
Minor roads are signed from St Austell. (Large carpark above beach.) There is a small sandy cove backed by cliffs where the contraband came in and the valley behind still provides a secluded route inland. Penrice House is still hidden in trees while Lobb's Shop is no more than a single house at the crossroads. Trewhiddle House, to the west, the probable base of John Copinger, is now a holiday centre.

Mevagissey
There is a large carpark at entry (others through narrow streets on the quay). Mevagissey is a fascinating working fishing port with lots of boats in the inner and outer harbours. An old boatbuilding shed on the quay is now a folk museum (open daily main season).

Gorran Haven
In a nest of narrow roads (but large carpark) Gorran Haven is small and quieter. Cottages cluster round a good sandy beach and small quay, protected by cliffs. Pass the Old Custom House on entry; see also the 16th century smuggling inn.

7
Falmouth and the Coast from Dodman Point to The Lizard

During the early 19th century the *Royal Cornwall Gazette* regularly published lists of seized contraband offered for public sale at Falmouth Custom House. One such sale runs:

650 lbs Pepper
266 lbs Chocolate
490 pairs Shoes
296 pairs Braces
66 pairs Pantaloons
181 pieces Ribbons, Galoons and Ferreting
59 dozen Shirt pins
21 pieces Nankeen
132 lbs Cheese
300 lbs Currants
30½ dozen Shawls
287 lbs Sugar
22 dozen Watch keys & chains
8 pieces Waistcoat shapes

On other occasions the public was invited to view and bid for bird seed, soap, tamarinds, feathers, hats, nails, bottles of castor-oil, Cologne and lavender water or Malta flower pots. The huge variety of contraband offered for sale is a clear indication that smuggling around Falmouth was of a different order from that generally practised in Devon and Cornwall. This difference is due to the special character of the magnificent sheltered stretch of deep water known as Carrick Roads,

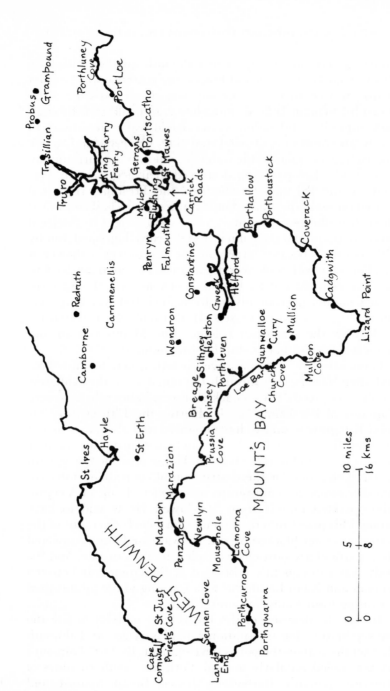

Places associated with the smuggling trade in south Cornwall.

which extends inland between Falmouth and St Anthony's Head. As at Dartmouth and Fowey, the entrance was fortified in the 16th century, but the gap was much too wide to be closed by a chain. Indeed smuggling craft could pass through with impunity, and sailing vessels could leave the estuary in nearly all conditions of wind and tide. Once inside Carrick Roads, fingers of navigable water fan out into the surrounding countryside. Before silting destroyed their access, even Tregony on the Fal and Tresillian on the Tresillian river had carried on seaborne trade. For centuries Truro had controlled all such traffic. As a stannary town with a right to the legal export of tin (and a huge illicit trade) Truro flourished, but by 1700 as vessels became larger and the Truro river shallower, it was Penryn which took over dominance. Penryn dates back to the 13th century and for hundreds of years was the westernmost Channel port supplying fresh food and water to merchant ships and naval vessels. It also built up an extensive trade with the American colonies, the Mediterranean and Scandinavia, and had a shipbuilding industry.

Falmouth was a comparative upstart, a new town developed after 1660 largely through the initiative of the Killigrew family, who lived at Arwenack House in Falmouth, and were Captains of Pendennis Castle. During the 17th century Sir John Killigrew is said to have financed and also participated in smuggling, as well as being implicated in piracy. A later Killigrew was to build the Custom House near the Quay, with its large chimney for the destruction of contraband tobacco. Another smuggler-cum-pirate was Robert Long of Veryan, who operated mainly from St Mawes. He is said to have brought his prizes into the Percuil (Porthcuel) river, one of the waterways later blocked by silt. He was caught and convicted for a particularly outrageous exploit in Veryan Bay, and his body was subsequently gibbetted at the crossroads between Veryan and Ruan Lanihorne as a warning to the pirates then operating from Lamorran on the Fal.

It was the decision of the Post Office in 1688 to site the Packet Station for international mail services at Falmouth that set the seal on the port's development. By 1702 Falmouth packets sailed regularly to New York, the southern states of America, Jamaica, Barbados, Mexico, Brazil, Spanish and 115

Portuguese ports, Malta and Madeira. There were 40 packet boats based at Falmouth by 1727, and more destinations were added when the West Indies sugar trade developed later. These were not cargo carrying vessels; they transported the mails and bullion. (There was a huge metal-lined safe cut into the hillside behind Falmouth, and covered wagons escorted by soldiers carried the valuables to London at a mere 3 mph!) The packet captains were well paid and were entitled to carry paying passengers. What mattered from a smuggling point of view was that the officers and crew could carry on their own private trading, and the vessels were exempt from searches by Customs men. This privilege was openly and grossly abused, until in 1785, at the insistence of the Customs, the Post Office established a commission to investigate the situation. It was found that the packets 'hovered' on both outward and homeward journeys, so that all on board could make maximum use of their privileged position. As a result the packet service was reorganised to prevent this smuggling. The crewmen had other ideas: they relied on their free enterprise profits to supplement their very inadequate pay, and so refused to put to sea. The Post Office was forced to raise their wages and pay a small food allowance before the packet service could be resumed. Not that this smuggling came to an end! In 1810 a zealous official inspecting two outwardbound packets broke open the seamen's private chests and seized their contents. Once more the men refused to put to sea, but the authorities responded by impressing 13 men from each crew into the Navy, a move which outraged local opinion. The Mayor was forced to read the Riot Act, a detachment of the Militia stood by, and the government temporarily transferred the packet service to Plymouth. In the end a compromise was agreed, but after 1820 the packets were forbidden to carry any such articles.

The packet captains chose to live at Flushing opposite Falmouth, and the past prosperity of this charming settlement is evident today. It owed its name to the Dutch engineers who came to build the quays and seawalls in the late 17th century. The women of Flushing became known for buying up the crewmen's contraband and carrying these private speculations to Truro or the mining settlements further inland. In this

Falmouth Harbour from a print by J M W Turner, which shows Pendennis Castle commanding the entrance to the sheltered waters of Carrick Roads. Reproduced by kind permission of the Cornish Studies Library, Redruth.

they were no doubt aided by an Excise clerk, convicted of fraud in 1822.

The packet boats were not the only opportunity for smuggling at Falmouth. Homeward bound vessels of the East India and West India Companies carried even more valuable and exotic cargoes, and Falmouth was the first port of call for almost all incoming merchant ships. The standard instruction to a ship's captain was 'to Falmouth for orders'. Naval vessels also crowded into Carrick Roads, and on at least one occasion there were as many as 350 seagoing ships in harbour at the same time. A fleet of little boats milled among them, carrying men, fresh supplies or further instructions and (of course) offloading whatever could be profitably traded.

Aside from these considerable opportunities, the winding creeks and wooded hillsides gave abundant scope for the more usual landings of spirits, tea and tobacco. Wool and tin were smuggled out; it was said that at one point three-quarters of Cornwall's tin was shipped out illegally. Bernard Wood reported that during the 1960s the Rev J V Hammond of St Just-in-Roseland pointed out from his garden overlooking the 117 river Fal where some of this had taken place. A favourite hiding place near Truro was at Penpol Farm, above Sunset Creek (opposite Malpas). Goods were carried up a sunken road and concealed in the local caves and woods. Mylor Creek, where there had once been a Royal Dockyard, seems to have been another depot, and a Riding Officer was based here. The Tresillian river, Tolverne near King Harry Ferry and Point on Restronguet Creek also figure in the smuggling records. At Penryn there is said to have been a tunnel leading from the foreshore to St Gluvias' vicarage. At Falmouth, beside two caves, there was a tunnel (now blocked) at Wells Beach. Swanpool Beach to the south on Falmouth Bay was a regular landing place, and there were confrontations between smugglers and preventivemen at Budock and Constantine to the west.

Along the open coast the whole way from Dodman Point to the Lizard are small beaches and undeveloped fishing villages which all took part in the trade. Starting in the north, the first is Porthluney Cove, beside Caerhays Castle. It was said that the gates of the estate were left open at appropriate times, and Richard Kingcup was one of the smugglers who ran goods here. Tenders were invited to build a Watch House at the small fishing village of Portloe, a sure sign of its illegal activities. Gerrans and Portscatho were similarly implicated.

South of Falmouth Bay the beautiful Helford river was navigable as far inland as Gweek, then the port for Helston. Gweek became a leading port for the export of tin and its general trade justified the establishment of a Custom House. It was also found necessary to base a preventive boat in Helford river by the 1820s. Frenchman's Creek (or Pill), a narrow finger of water on the south bank, had a reputation for smuggling, but no records appear to mention it. However, Mr J J Hill later recalled his boyhood on a Helford farm in the early 19th century. He joined a gang which operated from the small creek at Gillan, near Nare Point, and remembered that around 1850 two out of three ventures still proved successful.

The rocky coastline between the Helford river and the Lizard has always been isolated and remote from centres of population. The geology of this area is extremely interesting, and visitors today will be aware of the large roadstone quarries at Porthallow and Porthoustock. Both were fishing and smuggling settlements in the past. The fire-formed (igneous) and highly altered (metamorphic) rocks which outcrop in the cliffs here also form the dreaded Manacles Reef offshore. Coverack fishermen were caught smuggling on various occasions, and a preventive boat and later Coastguard Station were established here. At Cadgwith it was said in 1778: 'It is common for the inhabitants ... to take in and secrete smuggled goods for capital smugglers who frequently land cargoes'. Both Coverack and Cadgwith stand on Serpentine, an unusual and often beautiful rock, which weathers to produce the infertile and badly drained soil characteristic of Goonhilly Downs.

When it comes to the record of particular smuggling episodes, the story begins with another smuggling mayor. Captain Isaac Cocart, sometime Mayor of Falmouth, was caught in 1739 bringing in a large quantity of tea and other goods. Having been a smuggler, he later turned informer and was responsible for the conviction of a London merchant for smuggling tobacco. The authorities, being convinced of his change of heart, then sent him to Falmouth as master of a Revenue vessel, in the hope he would catch his former associates! Then during the 1760s homeward bound East Indiamen brought a series of smuggling bonanzas. In September 1762 three vessels arrived from China and stayed two weeks in Falmouth before a gunship from Plymouth arrived to escort them away. Hundreds of people came on foot or horseback to buy the exotic luxuries on offer through the private enterprise of the officers and crew. Choice fabrics, tea, arrack spirit and china were among the items for which it was believed some £20,000 was paid in total, draining the coffers of private individuals and Falmouth merchants alike. The Customs officers had some successes; in September 1762 they seized 27,579 lb of tea and 9,000 gallons of brandy, a haul large enough to justify a reward of £3,000. In 1765 another East Indiaman spent two weeks at Falmouth. The scene on board was described as like the busiest fair, seven days a week, and silks and muslins were hawked throughout the county. Meanwhile the more usual pattern of smuggling went on elsewhere, and 218 ankers of brandy were landed in one run at Porthoustock in 1762.

The struggle to restore law and order began in 1769 when Samuel Pellew was appointed Collector of Customs. He came from a distinguished seafaring family, and lived at Flushing. With his brother, Admiral Edward Pellew, he made determined efforts to stamp out the worst offences. The two brothers employed the Revenue cutters *Lark* and *Hawk*, but it was not until 17 years later that they defeated Wellard, the most notorious smuggler. Before that there was an ignominious occasion in 1774 when an Irish smuggling cutter chased the *Hawk* into Falmouth and then forced her boat on shore. Finally, in April 1786, the Pellews cornered Wellard on his ship *Happy-go-Lucky* in Mounts Bay. During the gun battle which followed Wellard was shot dead and several of the crew injured. The men surrendered and were imprisoned in Pendennis Castle. Thanks to the public attitudes of the time, all except the most severely injured man were freed by the townspeople, and when the remaining prisoner was brought to trial he was acquitted! Commenting on the prevalence of smuggling at Falmouth and especially up river at Truro, Warren Lisle reported: 'The Officers of all Ranks, too nearly related & too much connected, to give Offence to the Neighbouring Boroughs who always appoint' (which seems unfair to the Pellews!) Certainly smuggling around Falmouth continued, and on various occasions Danish vessels took part. In 1788 a Danish ship captained by an Englishman put into Falmouth but did not unload (because of Samuel Pellew's reputation). The captain then bought a 130 ton sloop, putting the second mate in charge of her. Both vessels then sailed out beyond the territorial limit in order to transship the cargo without interference. Finally the sloop ran the goods ashore at a less protected port.

Between 1796 and 1803 a whole series of captured vessels were brought into Falmouth by the combined efforts of the Revenue, Excise and naval ships. A number of these smuggling craft were registered at Fowey, and others were from Gweek, Polperro and Dartmouth. One vessel captured in 1796 was from Morlaix in Brittany, and described as 'marked for deception the *Poll of Jersey*', with a small swivel gun; she was manned by '18 stout fellows with blunderbus, musket, tomahawks and boarding pikes', no doubt because England and

France were at war! Cargoes were often large, for example, over 1,000 casks of spirits, and 3 tons 15cwt of tobacco in one case. One Fowey vessel had taken her cargo on board at sea from a neutral vessel, but the casks were reported to be 'just like those usually supplied, ready slung, from Guernsey'. The loss of so many specialised smuggling craft must have been depressing for the traders; some were now trying their luck with open rowboats. The *Sherborne Mercury* of 9th December 1799 advertised for sale at Gerrans the *Friend's Endeavour* sloop of 40 tons: 'will answer for the Guernsey trade, a very fast sailer'.

From time to time small seizures were made inland, but these must have represented a tiny fraction of the goods in transit. In August 1801 an Exciseman surprised a man carrying two ankers of brandy on horseback at King Harry Ferry. The man panicked with the result that the horse drowned, the rider escaped and the Exciseman got the brandy! Four years later in a similar minor triumph some brandy was seized on the Penryn to Truro mail coach, after the guard was seen stowing it in the boot. In a more serious incident the same year, three Excisemen were attacked by a dozen men 'in white frocks and trousers' who beat and stoned them, and rescued from them four horses loaded with stolen goods. It was common practice for the smugglers to try to repossess seized contraband. In one case a horse belonging to John Dunstone of Stithians (forfeited for being used to carry spirits) was stolen from a stable in Kerwyn Street, Truro. In similar fashion a large quantity of slates seized by a Gweek Customs man were stolen from a cellar in Helford in 1805. In 1823 officers seized 59 casks in a barn at Point, near Devoran. One man was left in charge while the others went to St Mawes. They returned to find four casks missing, and in the course of a search were set upon by a woman with a shovel and an innkeeper and his daughter (who claimed she had only been sowing seeds in her father's garden!) There must have been countless episodes of this type, but some had a serious outcome. In Mylor churchyard is a monument to Thomas James, aged 35, shot by a Customs officer on 7th December 1814, while returning in a boat from St Mawes to Flushing. Another violent encounter occurred 14 years later following a landing

121

A gravestone in Mylor churchyard in memory of Thomas James, shot by a
Customs Officer in December 1814.

at Swanpool. John Prior, Riding Officer at Falmouth and
Mr English the Riding Officer at Mylor met a gang of about
30 well armed smugglers at Constantine Church Town. A
serious battle ensued and Mr English was knocked unconscious and left for dead. The smugglers carried off their goods,
and the Board of Customs later offered a reward of £300 for
information leading to a conviction.

These were years when an astonishing variety of seized items was offered for sale at Falmouth Custom House. Apart from spirits, the lists included 13 pairs of pistols, 20 dozen packs of playing cards, 120 precious stones and one tiger skin! At Gweek in 1823 'an assortment of very elegant figured paper (containing 107 sheets for papering rooms)' was offered; one wonders where this went!

Many of the later seizures took place on the open coast at Portloe, Coverack or Gerrans Bay. The first Coastguard appointed at Coverack reported that despite his efforts 7,000 ankers of brandy had been run the previous year, and accordingly he asked for more help. The local smugglers' leader there was John Corylon, known for the red shirt his wife hung out on the washing line when the coast was clear. The Gerrans smugglers derived a particular advantage from the shape of the narrow isthmus leading south to St Anthony's Head. A lookout posted above the village could see down to the west into St Mawes harbour, and report on the activities of the preventive boat stationed there. On one occasion the local officer took his boat up the Percuil river and had it carried

The quay at Coverack, centre of operations for local smugglers' leader, John Corylon. In one year, 7,000 ankers of brandy were brought in despite the Coastguard's best preventive efforts.

123

over the low divide, so that it could be launched unexpectedly in Gerrans Bay, to catch the smugglers unawares. These cat-and-mouse tactics continued through the 1840s. A seizure in Penpol Woods above Sunset Creek had stopped one favourite hiding place, but Richard Kingcup and the notorious smuggler Ellery of Probus were still prepared to risk running goods in Truro river. One of the last recorded seizures was at Penryn in 1848.

PLACES TO VISIT

Falmouth
Explore the centre on foot! The Custom House (1820) faces the busy main street above the small original harbour and quay. The large brick-built chimney beside the Custom House was for burning contraband tobacco. The steam tug *St Denys* is moored at the quay and houses part of Falmouth Maritime Museum (open main season). Other displays featuring the Packet Service and Falmouth's maritime history are in Bell's Court (opposite Marks & Spencer) open daily. Arwenack House, the 17th century home of the Killigrew family, is at the south end of the main street. There are ferries to St Mawes and Flushing and boat trips from Prince of Wales Pier in the town centre. Pendennis Castle (Dept of Environment) affords excellent views from inside the grounds or from Castle Drive which encircles it. Swanpool Beach, (where landings were made) and other beaches are on the southern edge of the town.

Flushing and Mylor
These two attractive centres were very active in smuggling (limited parking only). Flushing village and quay face across to Falmouth. Named from 17th century Dutch builders of sea defences, Flushing boasts some handsome Queen Anne houses of packet ship captains. Mylor Churchtown has a modern yacht harbour and an ancient church with Norman doorways in a very attractive waterside setting. To find the monument to smuggler Thomas James shot in 1814, enter the churchyard from the waterside; the stone is where the path divides. There

is another granite memorial above the church with an amusing inscription to a local shipwright, Joseph Crapp, also a Cornish cross of the 5th century. Inside the church is a monument to Samuel Pellew, Collector of Customs. Also recommended is a visit to the 13th century thatched Pandora Inn at Restronguet Passage, the site of the ancient ferry to Feock.

Helford and Frenchman's Creek

Take the passenger ferry from Helford Passage, or drive through the maze of minor roads via Manaccan to the carpark south-east of Helford village. This beautiful spot with its thatched inn is a yachtsman's paradise. See Frenchman's Creek by water, or follow the signs to Kestle hamlet and walk down. Frenchman's Creek is the setting for Daphne du Maurier's romantic story of a French pirate who fell in love with the lady of the manor.

Portloe

This is the first of a series of tiny fishing villages on the open coast; all have limited parking and narrow roads, and all were smuggling centres. Portloe has a tiny harbour with a beach hemmed in by sharp upended schist-like cliffs. A scatter of whitewashed, slate-roofed houses is set back against the hillside. The Lugger Hotel is a modernised 17th century inn.

Gerrans and Porthscatho

Gerrans is the older centre, where the smugglers lived, and from which they could watch the Preventive boat based at St Mawes. Porthscatho is another quiet fishing village set in the wide sweep of Gerrans Bay, where there are several good beaches and lower cliffs.

Coverack

This charming and unspoilt fishing village has a tiny pier and good sands. Some of the attractive slate or thatched roofed cottages are known to have had hiding places below the floor. Coverack was the home of Jack Corylon, boatbuilder and smuggler, whose red shirt was an all clear signal when hung out to dry!

125

Cadgwith

Cadgwith is an attractive village with pink and white cottages (often thatched) on a steep and narrow road. In this area famed for its Serpentine rock, two shingle beaches are separated by a rocky promontory. A collapsed sea-cave, the Devil's Frying pan lies to the south. Once famous for pilchards, Cadgwith now depends on catches of crabs and lobsters. A small black building on the northern side of the cove (often referred to as a huer's hut) is the old Watch House.

8

The Iniquities of Mount's Bay and the Carters of Prussia Cove

'. . . In the western part of this County smuggling since the soldiers have been drawn off, has been carried on almost without control. Irish Wherries carrying 14, 16 or more guns and well manned, frequently land huge quantities of goods in defiance of the officers of the Customs and Excise, and their crews armed with swords and pistols escort smugglers a considerable distance from the sea, the smugglers themselves armed with offensive weapons and bidding defiance to all opposition which the officers can make, carry their goods from one part of the country to another almost every night. About a fortnight since a large Wherry landed according to the best information I can obtain from 1,500 to 2,000 ankers of spirits, about 20 tons of tea and other kinds of smuggled goods on a sandy beach in Mount's Bay, between Penzance and Marazion, near the public road, which whilst the goods were discharging was filled with armed men. . . . A few days after two officers got information that a very considerable quantity was concealed in the house and premises of a well known smuggler, obtained from me a search warrant, and were forcibly hindered from executing it by four men . . . I fear a criminal prosecution would be useless, at least for the reason it shocks me to mention, that a Cornish Jury would certainly acquit the smugglers. . . . These My Lord are the facts, it would be mere pedantry to attempt to describe to your Lordship the shocking effects, the moral and political consequences of smuggling carried to such a daring height, but I cannot help saying that perjury, drunkenness, idleness, poverty, contempt of the law, and an universal corruption of manners are in this neighbourhood too plainly seen to accompany it. It is [a] very unlucky circumstance that Patrick Plunkett who was lately discharged from our County gaol by an order from your Lordship, should have escaped without a prosecution. . . .'

This strongly worded letter was sent on 4th March 1778 to the Lord Chief Justice by the local squire, Edward Giddy of Tredrea Manor, just outside St Erth. He was evidently a Justice of the Peace and only too well aware of the problems. He was writing at a time when the Carter family had fortified their landing place and smuggling depot at Prussia Cove, and when any ship unfortunate enough to be driven on shore between Porthleven and Mullion would be stripped of cargo, sails, rigging or any other movable object within a matter of hours. Edward Giddy's comments echo those expressed by Customs officials throughout the 18th century, by Dr Borlase, author of *The Natural History of Cornwall* in 1755, and by a merchant from St Columb ten years later. It is often claimed

Penzance in 1817, from a contemporary print. Reproduced by kind permission of the Cornish Studies Library, Redruth.

that the smugglers of the West Country were much less violent than those of the South East. Certainly they were not guilty of sadistic cruelties which characterised the Hawkhurst Gang of Kent, but there was violence enough, and a virtual collapse of law and order. It is no surprise to find that Edward Pender, Mayor of Penzance, was bound over for smuggling in 1769. Public opinion in all levels of society was behind the smugglers. The one influential voice consistently and courageously ranged against this situation came from John Wesley. He first preached in Cornwall in 1743 and returned on more than 30 occasions. His teachings were to make a startling impact on Harry Carter, among others.

The Collector and his staff at the Customs House above the quay at Penzance were responsible for some 35 miles of vulnerable coastline, and sent a series of desperate requests for help. What was needed on land were soldiers based at the worst trouble spots, and in August 1740 some limited assistance was granted. Three officers and 25 privates were stationed at Penzance, a corporal and eight men at Marazion, four men at Newlyn and two at Mousehole. However, any deterrent effect was soon dissipated once these soldiers were withdrawn, leaving George Borlase to lament: 'The coasts here swarm with smugglers from Lands End to the Lizard, so that I wonder the soldiers . . . should have been ordered off without being replaced by others.' In 1763 there was a further request for six blunderbuses, six fusils, 20 pairs of pistols, 20 hangers (swords), two dozen tucks (for probing cargo) and two dozen lanterns. The virtual absence of roads at this time in west Cornwall added to the problems of controlling the area. By 1760 the first turnpike road from Truro had reached Marazion, but Penzance Corporation opposed its westward extension, so the public road Edward Giddy referred to must have been quite new.

There was an acute need for better vessels to patrol the sea; again desperate appeals for help went largely unheeded. In 1740 the Customs boat at Newlyn needed repairs estimated to cost £1.3.7d. Eight years later there was a request for a new boat at Marazion, estimated to cost £16, fully equipped and painted. And when at last the smuggling vessel *Speedwell* was captured and might have been employed in the service, the 129

Collector was ordered to burn the hull, sell the guns and ammunition to the highest bidder and remit the proceeds to London! Things were certainly no better in 1770 when the Collector reported they had seized very little due to the lack of a cutter, because the naval sloop which had been stationed there sailed very badly.

From the smugglers' point of view the situation looked very different. There was a ready market among the tin miners living close to the coast, and the tinners were happy to vary their hard existence by the occasional venture to Guernsey or Brittany. Mount's Bay faces directly towards these supply bases, and the inner north-west part of the bay (known as Gwavas Lake) was particularly sheltered and backed by gently sloping countryside. Because of the importance of Cornish tin for bronze smelting, trade with the Mediterranean world had begun in prehistoric times. Seven hundred years ago tin was exported legally or otherwise from Helston, but then the waves built up Loe Bar, cutting off direct access to the sea. As tin mining in west Cornwall became more important, Penzance was chosen in 1663 as the stannary town for the tin trade. By 1700 Penzance had developed a significant foreign trade in addition to its fishing and boatbuilding, and its harbour was improved several times during the 18th century. Little Mousehole, where pilgrims once waited for ships to take them to the Holy Land, was then a much more important fishing port than Newlyn. Ships from Mousehole carried pilchards to France and the Mediterranean, and brought back the salt needed in their processing. (Martha Blewett was murdered in 1792 for the money she made selling untaxed salt.)

It was plainly imprudent to land contraband under the eyes of Penzance Custom House, so the favourite landing beaches throughout the 18th century were between Marazion and Porthleven or near Mullion. Here the coast is more exposed and often backed by cliffs, but there are many secluded coves where a landing could take place unobserved. The most famous of these are the three tiny coves east of Cudden Point: Prussia Cove, Piskies Cove and Bessy's Cove, the home base from which the Carter family smuggled for over 40 years. Porthleven, at the northern end of Loe Bar, had an unenviable reputation for both wrecking and smuggling. The first proper harbour here was completed in 1818, but totally destroyed by the sea in 1824. It was immediately rebuilt, despite being dangerously exposed to the prevailing winds, and there were further improvements later. A tunnel is reported to have led from caves west of the harbour up to Methleigh Manor, with storage under the kitchen floor. Sithney, two miles inland, was apparently a gang headquarters and also had storage. Another depot was discovered at Wendron (during road widening in 1905). A properly constructed tunnel 33 ft long linked six chambers, each 6 ft by 9 ft; it was found clean, dry and empty!

Gunwalloe Fishing Cove at the southern end of Loe Bar was the next recognised landing site. A tunnel is said to have linked a cave on the beach to the belfry tower, and other caves were used for storage. Another passage is believed to have linked the cove to the Halzephron Inn. At Halzephron House (almost on the clifftop) a tunnel leading to the cliff face is now covered with a metal grill. A nice story tells how Henry Cuttance, a local smuggler, escaped from the Man-of-War

Mullion Cove, once celebrated for its pilchards – and smuggling. The notorious smuggler Wellard was killed in a fight offshore here in 1786.

onto which he had been press-ganged by throwing his hat over one side, shouting 'man overboard', and then diving over the other! The small beaches at Church Cove, Poldhu Cove and Polurrian Cove were certainly used for landings, and the goods carried up through Cury, but Mullion Cove is the one most often mentioned in the records. Once called Porth Mellin, it lies at the heart of spectacular scenery where the sea has carved cliffs, offshore stacks and caves into the dark green Serpentine rock. The pilchard fishery here was very important, but the local vicar, Rev E G Harvey wrote in 1875 that almost every family was involved in smuggling in the 18th and early 19th centuries. Houses in Mullion village had all the usual secret shafts, chambers in walls, concealment under floors and behind cupboards with false backs. Moreover, the people were proud to have taken part in what they termed 'the smuggling *service*'! According to Hippisley Coxe, the smugglers Bobo George and John Munday used Torchlight Cave for storage, and a tunnel led up to a clifftop farm.

There were other small landing beaches among the granite cliffs of West Penwith. At Lamorna Cove, where vessels could be beached, the local inn is called 'The Wink' (a regular term for an unlicensed alehouse where spirits might be had 'under the counter'). Porthcurno figures in the smuggling records, and at Porthgwarra there are said to have been two tunnels leading up from the cove to the hamlet above. Beyond Land's End were two more landing places facing onto the open Atlantic. Sennen Cove in the early 19th century was regularly used for landings of contraband as well as red mullet and pilchards. Priest's Cove, immediately below Cape Cornwall, was the tiny harbour serving the tin mining centre of St Just-in-Penwith. Significantly there was another inn here called 'The Wink' which certainly served the local tinners in more boisterous times.

Unhappily the 18th century Custom House records start with stories of wrecking, and a few examples show what happened. In 1738 the *Vigilante* from Hamburg was driven ashore near Perran Uthnoe, and despite help from soldiers quartered locally, the wreckers took not only the cargo but the sails and rigging. The following year the *Lady Lucy* was wrecked at Gunwalloe in the early hours of the morning and the cargo – 68 tuns of wine, 25 tons of coffee berries, 18 casks of indigo and 31½ 'pieces' of brandy – had all vanished before the Customs officers arrived. When later the local houses were searched, the Vicar of Cury was found to have secreted some of the wine casks! In December 1748 the *Jonge Alcida* from Bordeaux was wrecked near Porthleven when bound for Amsterdam with a cargo of wine. Customs officials tried to rescue this, but 'the violence and barbarity of the country people was such that they could not save one cask and ran a hasard of their lives in the attempt'.

In the 1750s and 1760s the Penzance Collector could seldom report seizures of goods; more usually he wrote of officers fearful of being knocked on the head, of break-ins and thefts from the Customs warehouse or other violence. In 1751 a late night confrontation in Penzance led to 'a gore of blood', but the worst episode occurred in March 1768 when William Odger (or Odgers), stationed at Porthleven, was murdered when he and another officer attempted to seize smuggled goods. A reward of £100 was offered for information leading to a conviction, and warrants were issued for the arrest of Melchisedeck Kinsman and three other men. Two were believed to have taken refuge at Morlaix in Brittany, and the others in Guernsey. Meanwhile, the principal witness for the Crown dare not go to work. Accordingly he was granted a pension, and was still drawing 10 shillings a week when he died 20 years later. Eventually Melchisedeck Kinsman was caught and his three companions surrendered. All were then tried for the murder of Odger, but found not guilty!

The Customs officers were scoring at least limited successes, and the sales of contraband brought in an average of £1,200 a year during the 1760s. In 1772 the *Duchess of Buccleugh* proved a more interesting prize, with a cargo that included 5,121 silk handkerchiefs, 220 yards of black lace, three parcels of silk and eleven pincushions! In 1780 and again two years later substantial quantities of tea were found under beds and in haystacks at Sithney. Then in 1788 a puncheon of rum was washed ashore, rescued by an officer and stored in the Penzance warehouse. Lord Arundel claimed this under his ancient rights to flotsam and jetsam, and the Collector sought advice from the Board in London.

133

Throughout these years the catalogue of violence continued. In 1771 a naval officer and crewman were violently threatened at Mousehole. The next year the Penzance Custom boat was sabotaged and sunk. In 1775 three armed Irish wherries anchored for three days close to the port, defiantly discharging contraband, and the Collector was powerless to intervene. Five years later all the Customs men at Mousehole were charged with accepting bribes and actively assisting smuggling. In 1782 the fatally injured body of a Customs boatman was found on the beach at Marazion, and two years later James Richards, Excise officer at St Michael's Mount, was knocked down by a stone and died two months later. The only sign of successful opposition came in 1786 when the Pellew brothers from Falmouth, sailing in two Revenue vessels, surprised and shot dead the notorious smuggler Wellard when his ship was anchored off Mullion. The other saga of these years concerns the Carter family of Prussia Cove.

John Carter, the self-styled 'King of Prussia', and his brother Henry (or Harry) are unquestionably the best known Cornish smugglers. This is largely because Harry Carter wrote his autobiography in 1809, which was published with introductory notes by the solicitor John B Cornish in 1894. In his account Harry was careful to protect those members of the family firm who were still smuggling (he calls them the Cove Boys.) In consequence one has to look to official reports and contemporary newspapers to learn more about John Carter and the other family members. Harry was an able man, ambitious, self disciplined, intensely religious and with a strong but complex moral code. He may have been neurotic, and his writing refers to his 'conchance' staring him in the face! He can hardly have been popular with his less religious crewmen.

Various Carter families are known to have lived in Cornwall at least since the mid 16th century, and the forebears of John and Harry lived in the Breague and Germoe areas. Francis Carter, father of ten children, most of whom became smugglers, was not a seafaring man. He worked as a miner and also rented a smallholding at Pengersick (Praa Sands), where Henry was born in 1749. The members of the family firm are more fully listed in Appendix III, but the most important were John, the second son born in 1738, known as the 'King of Prussia', and Henry (or Harry) the seventh child. Apart from two who died in childhood, and Ann, whose husband Richard Champion joined the gang, all the seven sons were involved in the trade to some degree. Francis, the fifth child and the two youngest, Roger and Charles, took an active part. The family grew up in what Harry calls decent poverty; only John and Charles (the youngest) received much education, and the others went to work as soon as possible.

Smugglers Alarmed, a popular print of the early 19th century.

135

Harry later educated himself (he started with the necessary discipline of keeping accounts!) and the phonetic spellings of his autobiography add to its interest. Harry worked at the local mine from the age of nine or ten, but then joined two of his older brothers fishing and smuggling. John Carter may have adopted his title from a childish game (Frederick the Great's reputation was considerable at this time). He was the organiser of the gang and rented what had been known as Porth Leah, but was soon called King's Cove or Prussia Cove. There are in fact three small coves; the most westerly is Piskies Cove, Bessy's Cove is the central one and the most secluded, and was named after Bessy Bussow who kept an alehouse or 'wink'. Both these coves face south and are sheltered by Cudden Point. King's Cove faces east and is immediately north of Enys islet. By 1770, when he was 33, John was prosperous enough to build a substantial stone dwelling known as King's House on the clifftop above King's Cove. It stood directly above a large cave. John cut a proper harbour and roadway, adapted the caves for storage and established a battery on the headland between King's Cove and Bessy's Cove. Today the most obvious signs of these activities can be seen in Bessy's Cove, where there are wheel ruts worn into the stone platform of the beach, and other clear signs of a roadway. From a cave at the back of the beach a secret passage led up to Bessy's alehouse (later extensively altered and now called Cliff Cottage). The King's House which John built in 1770 was demolished in 1906, to be replaced by the present private mansion, and its drive runs over the King's House site.

It is clear that the family firm was having great successes in the 1760s and 1770s, and John had a reputation for his own brand of honesty. A story is told about the occasion when John returned to the cove to find that an Exciseman had carried off the cargo he was due to deliver to his customers. Judging that his reputation for prompt and honest service was at stake, he went with armed companions and broke open the Penzance Customs store, but took only his own casks, leaving those belonging to others.

Harry joined his older brothers in their smuggling enterprise in 1766, but soon sailed with other (perhaps more experienced) crews from Folkestone and Ireland. He got on well, and by the time he was 25 he already had his own vessel, soon to be replaced by a larger one. As he says 'My success was rather beyond common, and after a time we bought a small cuttar of aboute 50 tons and aboute ten men'. All his voyages at this stage proved successful; his puritanical outlook was already evident, and no swearing was allowed among his crew. The Carters evidently found it paid them to own their vessels rather than hire others to carry their cargoes. The War of American Independence, which lasted from 1775 to 1783, provided great opportunities to combine smuggling with privateering, for those with sufficient capital and standing in the community. To obtain the necessary Letter of Marque, a ship's papers had to be in order, and its armament registered; the owners had also to provide a bond. An armed privateer was then entitled to seize enemy shipping, and the crew could not be impressed into the Navy. The Carter family firm was able to obtain Letters of Marque for at least five vessels during these years (they are listed in Appendix III). The two largest were the 200 ton *Swallow*, owned by John and captained in 1777 by Harry, with 16 big guns, 26 swivel guns and a crew of 60, and the *Shaftesbury*, also of 200 tons, armed with 16 big guns and 12 swivels, carrying a crew of 80 and commanded in 1780 by Harry. (The owners were listed as John, Edward and Harry Carter and Richard Champion.)

So by the time he was 28 Harry had command of one of the largest cutters afloat. As he wrote: 'we gained a large sum of money, and being a speculating family were not satisfied with small things'. He adds that they presently expected to make £10,000. But smuggling was always a high risk occupation, and Harry now became the victim of international conflicts. He took his new cutter to St Malo for repairs, but was thought to be a pirate because he was not carrying proper documentation, and was put in gaol. (He writes movingly of the horrors of clanging doors and jangling keys, but presently settled down to teach himself navigation.) His brother John came over to seek his release, but both were held until they were exchanged for two Frenchmen, through the intervention of the Lords of the Admiralty. (This can only mean that the Carters had friends in very high places!) They returned without the 137 new cutter, and found the family firm in low water, but because of their reputations got immediate credit from Guernsey merchants. Harry was soon off again in a small cutter taking contraband to Mumbles in South Wales. While he was negotiating the sale on shore, his vessel was mistaken for a privateer, and the crew had to cut her cable and put to sea. Harry was left behind without papers and was yet again detained under suspicion of piracy. Once more the Lords of the Admiralty negotiated his release, and Harry went back to very successful smuggling.

It was evidently at Christmas in 1782 when Harry was at Newquay with two of the family privateers, the *Shaftesbury* (which he commanded) and the *Phoenix*, commanded by Ralph Dewen, that he received a request from the Collector of Customs (apparently John Knill of St Ives) to attack the enemy privateer *Black Prince* from Dunkirk, which had been causing great trouble in the Bristol Channel. Most of the men had gone ashore, and Harry had difficulty collecting sufficient crew, but this was a request he felt compelled to answer. With his two vessels he pursued and attacked the *Black Prince*. The privateer tried to take refuge in Padstow, but in the end the captain abandoned his sinking ship, and Harry Carter managed to rescue 17 of the 31 men on board.

In 1786 Harry married Elizabeth Flindel from Helford, and their daughter Betsy was born the following year. Disaster struck during January 1788, when Harry took a cargo into Cawsand. He gives a detailed account of what happened. His brother Charles was in the landing party, but Harry had not been warned that a Man-of-War was in the area. As the hatches were opened ready for the landing, two open boats appeared. Too late it was realised that these had not come to land the cargo but were from a naval frigate. Harry's vessel was boarded and hand to hand fighting took place. The crewmen on deck threw away their weapons and fled, but ten men trapped below decks were captured. Harry apparently put up a desperate single-handed fight before being very badly wounded and left for dead on deck. Miraculously he later lowered himself into the shallows, managed to reach the beach, and was rescued by the landing party and his brother Charles. Despite terrible wounds to his face and skull, he left with

Charles the following night by chaise (the doctor came with them as far as Lostwithiel). Harry spent a week in Charles' house at Kenneggy, but then a reward of £300 was advertised for information leading to his capture. To escape arrest he took refuge with a gentleman of Marazion, and then hid in Acton Castle nearby. This had recently been built by Mr John Stackhouse, Fellow of Exeter College, Oxford and owner of Pendarves House. He had intended to use Acton Castle in connection with his researches into seaweeds. John Carter, as his tenant and near neighbour, acted as caretaker and had a key. (John Stackhouse can hardly have been ignorant of the Carter's regular profession!) Harry took various precautions to avoid detection, and the doctor who attended him was brought there blindfold.

The story as Harry tells it is highly significant, but he is also being economical with the truth. Clearly he owed his freedom to some powerful friends, but had his crime been no more than landing contraband at Cawsand, he would not have found a price of £300 on his head. Official records and the *Exeter Flying Post* of 31st January 1788 tell a different story. When Harry's vessel *Revenge* came into Cawsand she was seen by the Revenue cutter *Busy*, and the naval frigate *Druid* was informed. Two boats from the *Druid* manned by armed naval seamen went to intercept the smugglers. In the ensuing battle one seaman was killed and a number of others wounded. So Harry Carter and his crew were as guilty of murder as were the men on the *Lottery* who shot Humphrey Glynn. No wonder Harry came to regard himself as a desperate sinner who needed to fast and mortify the flesh! His ten arrested crewmen were all impressed into the Navy. But to continue the story as he tells it, after three months he had recovered sufficiently to walk over to Prussia Cove at night to meet the 'Cove Boys'. Moreover, the time limit for the £300 reward had expired, so he was in less immediate danger. That summer his wife developed consumption, and by October she was dying. It was decided that Harry should go to America (the family sent money to maintain him), so he sadly took leave of his wife, and sailed to New York by way of Leghorn and Barcelona. There he became a Methodist convert, and at one stage did casual farm work on Long Island, including working among

139

Bessy's Cove, at Prussia Cove, home of the best known Cornish gang, the Carter family. Part of the roadways cut by John Carter can be seen on the left, and there are wheelruts cut in the rock of the beach. Bessy's alehouse (now much enlarged and improved) stands above some caves on the right of the picture.

negro slaves. Finally in September 1790 he got a passage back to Dunkirk on a ship flying American colours, and was soon back with his brother Charles at Kenneggy.

As an important Methodist convert, Harry was now persuaded to preach locally, but then at Helston 'a great man of the neighbourhood' warned him to disappear before others betrayed him. The family firm then arranged for him to go as their agent to join the colony of smugglers' merchants and other expatriates in Roscoff. (It took 15 hours in an open boat from Prussia Cove.) For a time all went well, and Harry preached regularly to the English community, but in 1793 war broke out between England and France, and Harry and many others were put under house arrest. His account of the privations of imprisonment under the Reign of Terror brings home the horror of this period in France, under the shadow of the guillotine. One touching episode was Harry's struggle to talk French to the Carmelite nuns who shared his incarceration. But he also came to know well several of the wealthy smugglers' merchants, in particular Mr Clancie, Mr Diot and Mr and Mrs Macculloch. He was finally freed in January 1795 and returned to Cornwall that August, and a great family reunion. John Carter and the 'Cove Boys' were still at Prussia Cove, Charles was at Kenneggy and Francis at Rinsey. Harry's autobiography ends at this point, and he was careful not to implicate his brothers, who were still carrying on the family tradition. Having abandoned his own part in this, Harry was now short of money. In Cornwall Record Office is the bond, dated 18th April 1799, whereby 'Henry Carter of Penhale, Breague, yeoman' undertook to repay £326.19.8d (with interest) to James Macculloch of Gulval, on or before 18th April 1800. For the remaining years of his life he lived quietly on a smallholding at Rinsey, and acted as a Methodist lay preacher. When he died, aged 80 in 1829, he left all his possessions to his friend James Macculloch, to whom he was still in debt. His full will is set out in Appendix IV.

During Harry's enforced absence in France, the authorities made great efforts to destroy the Carter stronghold. In 1792 it was reported that stores in Prussia Cove held 40 gallons of rum, 739 of brandy and 2,778 of gin, a huge quantity of spirits, and that this was protected by eight six-pounder guns. Two years later the Penzance Collector managed to get help from the Helston and Penzance Volunteer batallion, who went down into the cove and fired on the battery. They took it by direct assault, dismounted the guns, and tried to recover goods on a wrecked vessel there. They were violently opposed by the local population, who pelted them with stones. A Marazion doctor helped the smugglers throughout, giving the initial warning and joining in the defence of the battery. One officer was shot through the cheek, and the volunteers were compelled to fire on the crowd, before seizing what they could – a mere eight casks of brandy and five of gin – and departing. They were forced to leave large quantities of spirits, tea, tobacco and snuff on the beach. Warrants were issued to arrest the leading smugglers, but no constable would enter the cove unless protected by the military. The commanding officer of the troops stationed at Helston refused to go in without direct orders from the War Office!

So the smuggling went on; John Carter's son-in-law, Will 141

SMUGGLING IN DEVON AND CORNWALL

Richards, took over at some stage. On one occasion he nearly burned down the house when he threw straw and chaff onto the fire to make the necessary signal to an incoming vessel. In 1801 another vessel masquerading as a coaster sailed boldly past the *Dolphin* Revenue cutter, and then began to land goods too early, and was spotted from St Michael's Mount. One hundred ankers of spirits were seized at the cove, but the vessel slipped away with the rest of the cargo.

John Carter, the 'King of Prussia', died in 1803 and in May of that year the lease of Prussia Cove was offered for sale. The sale particulars describe 'All those large and commodious Cellars, Lofts, Salt-Houses, Fish-Presses, Boat-Beds, Capstan . . . Together with the said Cove and Landing Places therein. The above premises are exceedingly well adapted and situate for carrying on any kind of trade. . . .' Despite this it seems clear that the family firm continued in business at least until a preventive boat was based here; after 1825 a characteristic row of Coastguard cottages looked down on King's Cove and Battery Point!

The end of smuggling at Prussia Cove marks a turning point. Smugglers had increasingly to rely on guile rather than force, most cargoes were sunk offshore for later retrieval, and remoter shores at Sennen and St Just, as well as the Mullion beaches were increasingly used. Mr J A D Bridger published several stories (from briefs prepared by a local solicitor) which show how farmers and innkeepers carried on the trade around 1805. Thomas Hicks, innkeeper at St Just-in-Penwith had evidently collected £100 in bank notes and other bills to purchase goods from a lugger lying offshore at Priest's Cove. Unfortunately, the open boat in which he and seven Polperro men from the lugger were coming ashore was upset in the heavy surf, and he and four other men were drowned. Some £50 of the money invested by his customers was recovered. On two later occasions spirits and tobacco were found concealed in mine workings at St Just, and on the second occasion (in 1828) one of the preventivemen fell to his death down the shaft.

At Sennen there were similar enterprises. Dionesius Williams, a wealthy farmer from Mayon above Sennen Cove, owned the Sennen Inn and provided the capital for smuggling ventures. His tenant at the inn (said to be a resort of black-guards) was John George, who landed the cargoes for him. When John George failed to pay the rent, farmer Williams turned him out, whereat George's wife Ann turned King's Evidence, and Dionesius Williams was heavily fined. Ann George also turned King's Evidence against another well-to-do farmer, Christopher Pollard of Madron. He had a previous conviction for smuggling and had fled to France to escape imprisonment. Pollard was accused of inciting a crowd of 300 or 400 people to recapture contraband on Sennen Beach, of using foul language and striking an Excise officer. The officers were defending 1,000 gallons of brandy and the same quantities of rum and gin, and 500 lb of tobacco (a huge haul with suspiciously round numbers!) He was acquitted, but ultimately imprisoned for smuggling off Plymouth. The third case in 1815, which involved innkeeper Oats of St Just and farmer Permewan of Trevear, Sennen, has already been told in Chapter 2. A much smaller smuggling venture ran into more trouble. Smugglers in the *Rose* of Coverack brought 200 tubs from Roscoff and tried to land these at Gunwalloe, but were warned off. They then went to Porthcurno and got 50 ashore before a blue light indicated trouble. The landing party hid behind a hedge and then carried the spirits past Treen village to Tressider Bottoms. The place under the mill was full, so the cargo was hidden in the furze. The local farmer helped, and the incriminating tubs were got rid of in 'Burga Churchtown'. (This may be St Buryan.)

At the other end of Mount's Bay things were becoming difficult at Mullion, where a Coastguard station was established after 1824. Some landings were at awkward sites – The Chair, south of Mullion (where an adit mine was used for storage), or at Angrowse Cliffs to the north. Many tubs were crept up by the preventive services, and one Coastguard claimed he had charge of 800 tubs on one occasion. However, in 1847 all but one of the tubs was successfully carried up through Cury after what was probably the last significant landing here. Two final episodes were recorded at Gulval (beside today's Heliport) in 1848, and in the streets of Penzance itself at 11 pm on 10th July 1851; the end of a violent period.

143

PLACES TO VISIT

Since virtually every beach and settlement along this coast
was involved in the trade, one is spoilt for choice! The most
closely implicated include:

Mullion and Poldhu Coves
Families providing the 'smuggling service' lived at Mullion
village itself. (Signed carpark for the Cove beside road down
at SW 672181.) Mullion's tiny harbour is enclosed by solid
granite piers, amongst magnificent cliffs and stacks cut in
Serpentine rock. There are excellent cliff walks along the coast
path in both directions. To the north is Polurrian Cove, with
its delightful beach and Poldhu Cove, reached via a minor
road from Mullion village, has good sands and a valley
leading straight back to Cury. (Roadside parking at SW
668200.) Poldhu Cove still looks the perfect spot to run a
cargo! Cury church, where the parson took part in wrecking,
has a Norman doorway. The monument to Marconi on the
summit of Angrouse Cliffs commemorates the first radio mes-
sage sent to Newfoundland in December 1901. The coast path
north of Poldhu Cove leads over to Gunwalloe, but there is no
road connection. Somewhere offshore here smuggler Wellard
was shot dead during a fight with the Pellew brothers in 1786.

Gunwalloe Cove
Approach by car from the north along a minor road off A3083,
3 miles south of Helston. Pass Gunwalloe Fishing Cove and
Halzephron Cliff to the carpark at SW 659209. The first
church here was built in AD 570 and dedicated to the Breton
saint, Winwaloe. The present church is 14th and 15th century
and under attack from the sea and blown sand; it has a
separate belfry built into rock. Apart from smuggling, these
beaches are noted for treasure hunting. Emery, a 17th century
buccaneer, is said to have buried his wealth here; a Portuguese treasure ship was wrecked here in 1526 and another
vessel carrying 2½ tons of Spanish dollars in 1785. There have
been various unsuccessful efforts to find this treasure, but a
storm in 1912 brought to light Spanish gold coins buried in
144   Loe Bar!

Porthleven
This is still something of a working port which once had delusions of grandeur! There are some older buildings round the harbour but the seafront was damaged by storms once again early in 1990. The minor road running east along the coast passes Coastguard cottages and leads to a carpark at SW 636249 near the entrance to the Penrose Estate and Loe Bar. There are delightful lakeside walks in the Penrose Estate and some signs of former mining. Loe Pool is believed to have inspired Tennyson's story of Excalibur. Loe beach was notorious for wrecking and smuggling. HMS *Anson* was wrecked on Loe Bar in 1807, and Henry Trengrouse of Helston developed a rocket life-saving apparatus as a result.

Prussia Cove
From A394 in Rosudgeon take the narrow road signed to Prussia Cove and the carpark near the clifftop at SW 554283. Access can be gained from here to the coast path between Bessy's Cove and Enys Islet, though the coves themselves are on private property. It is in Bessy's Cove that one can see the roadways built by John Carter and wheel ruts cut into the rocks of the shore, below high tide mark. Some of the storage caves are obvious. A shaft up from the beach is now blocked but once emerged beside an iron-roofed shed. Bessy's alehouse has been extended and altered to become Cliff Cottage. John Carter's house stood above King's Cove further to the northeast, where the residence built in 1906 now stands. There is a good view of St Michael's Mount from Cudden Point to the west. The Carters fortified Battery Point east of Bessy's Cove. The coast path leads round to the Coastguard cottages and Kenneggy, where Charles lived, and on to Praa Sands. Another minor road off A394 at Ashton leads down to Rinsey, where Harry ended his days, and a carpark at Rinsey Head. There is a fine stretch of coast path between here and Trewarvas Head on National Trust land, and the engine house of Wheal Prosper Mine.

Mousehole (pronounced Mowzle)
This quaint but congested fishing village with its tiny harbour is one of the most evocative smuggling centres in West Pen- 145

with. It was in the narrow lane up to Paul that Martha Blewett was murdered in 1792 for the money she earned selling uncustomed salt.

Lamorna Cove and Porthcurno

Lamorna Cove at the foot of a narrow valley is one of the obvious landing sites in West Penwith. Another further west is along the sandy beach at Porthcurno. A large carpark here serves both the beach and the Minack open-air theatre. The famous Logan Rock is on a headland to the east.

Sennen Cove

Sennen Cove lies at the south end of magnificent Whitesand Bay. Close to Land's End, and partially sheltered by a rocky headland to the west, the glorious sandy beach extends north to Aire Point, peppered with massive granite boulders. Prevailing winds sweep the sandhills against the cliff face. The old centre of Sennen village stands astride A30 on the plateau inland. Between the village and the minor road down to the separate settlement at Sennen Cove is Mayon Farm, home of at least one smuggling entrepreneur. (Main Cove carpark at SW 356263, and others beside Life Boat Station and jetty.) With its old inn and fishermen's cottages it is not difficult to visualise fighting here between smugglers and preventive men during the early 19th century. A cache of drugs was picked up on this beach in March 1990!

9

The Surfing and Holiday Beaches of North Cornwall

Once past Cape Cornwall, the coast runs north-eastwards to the county boundary and Hartland Point beyond. The total distance along the coastal footpath is almost 134 miles, and very much more along the actual indented shoreline. The varied and magnificent scenery delights today's visitors, but this was always a hostile environment for the sailor dependent on wind and tide. The section north of the Camel river was particularly feared:

> 'From Hartland Point to Padstow Light
> Is a watery grave by day or night.'

A characteristic feature of the scenery of north Cornwall is the plateau-like character of much of the interior. Erosion over millions of years has left a platform at around 430 ft above sea level, into which streams have cut deep valleys, often a most attractive feature of the landscape, and useful as secluded routeways for carrying contraband inland! The even summit level of the cliffs seems at odds with the violent folds and contortions of the rocks exposed along the shore or in the cliff face, particularly between Boscastle and Hartland Point. Coastal erosion has etched out every weakness in the rocks to produce caves and arches, offshore islets and secluded coves. The smugglers knew them all! Further south the toughest rocks stand out as headlands: the igneous, or fire-formed granite and greenstone of West Penwith and lavas at Pentire Point north of the Camel; hard sandstones or rocks baked

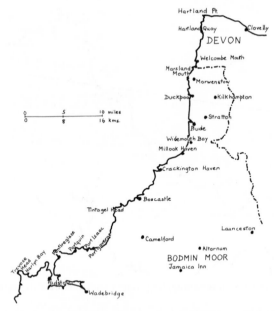

Places associated with the smuggling trade in north Cornwall: north section.

when the granite masses were injected amongst them at Godrevy Point and St Agnes Head; or tough grits near Newquay. Where the less resistant slates come to the coast, the sea has cut the bays so popular today. The largest of these, St Ives, Perran and Watergate Bays, lie open to the prevailing winds, and the glorious sandy beaches are backed by dunes built up over many centuries – an open invitation to clandestine landings from small boats! Moreover, this sand is rich in lime, a natural fertiliser for the acid soils of north Cornwall. Accordingly, for centuries sand and seaweed were carried inland by pack animals along sunken 'sandways', to be spread on upland fields. The system could be readily modified to carry other goods! In the Newquay and Padstow areas in particular teams of mules or donkeys were recruited for the task, sometimes taught opposite words of command and with their backs greased to make capture more difficult! Later short canals were built to carry sand, seaweed or coal inland, and though no firm evidence exists, it seems highly probable that the smugglers appropriated this form of transport also. At

148

Places associated with the smuggling trade in north Cornwall: south section.

Bude a canal, completed in 1824, linked the coast to the Tamar valley and beyond, using an inclined plane to reach the summit level. Near Newquay a wealthy St Columb merchant called Edvean devised a different system. A horizontal canal at almost 200 ft high ran inland from the clifftop north of Mawgan Porth, and a derrick was used to raise the goods to this level through a shaft dug close to the cliff edge. (Bob Acton's guide to walks round Newquay gives precise instructions for finding part of the canal bed west of Trenance, and reaching both the top and bottom of the shaft.) There was a second, lower canal which started behind Lusty Glaze beach at Newquay leading eastwards, but the full scheme failed because water leaked from the canals.

Hiding places to store contraband were readily available. In addition to numerous coastal caves, mining activity had created vertical shafts and horizontal adits (for drainage) which honeycomb the cliffs near St Agnes, Perranporth and Newquay in particular. The Cornish word for cave is 'vugga' or 'vouggha', and this is also related to the word 'fougou', used for artificially cut underground passages or storage places of prehistoric origin. (The latter may have been used as 149

Caves at Perranporth in cliffs riddled with mine workings which the smugglers used to store contraband.

primitive larders, but their exact purpose is unknown.) In 1961 an underground storage place was discovered at Treveglos Farm, Zennor in West Penwith, which was confidently described as a smugglers' hiding place. There were signs that goods had been hauled out using ropes or chains and it had apparently been opened in the 1920s, but this may have originally been a fougou. S A Opie, writing in the 1930s, listed a series of caves and tunnels cut into the subsoil of Carnmenellis, south of Redruth. Unquestionably the smugglers used some if not all of these, but they were probably intended for farm use.

The great smugglers' vugga at Porthcothan, west of Padstow is entirely authentic however, and included both a main storage cavern and one (or possibly two) smaller entry tunnels. It is on private land, difficult to find and has now largely fallen in, so we must rely on the descriptions given by the Rev S Baring-Gould in a *Daily Graphic* article of November 1894 and in his *Book of the West, Vol 2 Cornwall* of 1899. The entrance is about a mile from the coast, up the little valley leading south-east towards Penrose, in the side valley branching to the south, with steep sides covered with gorse. Some 350 yards along this side valley, and rather more than half way down its steep west side is a concealed hole, just large enough to enter stooping. Inside there are notches where a beam could be fixed to bar the entrance. The tunnel becomes larger inside, being up to 8 ft 3 ins wide, and from 7 ft 6 ins to 8 ft 6 ins high, and runs west for 50 ft. A lower side gallery branches off 7 ft from the entrance and was still (when Baring-Gould explored it) 17 ft long, but had partly fallen in. It once led to Treveme-dar (or Trevethen in the 1899 version), emerging in a cottage garden there. Baring-Gould claimed this once extended for 3,500 ft (about 1 km), curving round in a wide sweep, and provided with air and peep holes. He declared the whole excavation was cut out of solid rock, with pick marks discerni-ble, and expressly made for smuggling; the date 1747 was cut at the end. An old woman told him that her father remem-bered the tunnel 'filled wi' casks of run spirit right chuck-full'. The Porthcothan carpark attendant around 1982 could still speak of his great grandfather's involvement in what went on, and the vugga was used for storage in the Second World War. Its secret was never discovered!

These shores were not easy to reach from Roscoff or Guern-sey; instead it was Irish vessels bringing cargoes from the storehouses at Rush, north of Dublin, which feature strongly in the smuggling story along this coast and its continuation in north Devon. All the contemporary accounts speak of Irish wherries, small open-decked sailing vessels with a shallow draught, well suited to these difficult waters. When in the late 18th century larger and faster Revenue craft began to mount successful opposition, the Irish smuggling companies, too, invested in larger and more powerfully armed ships. By that time fine new vessels from Fowey and the Channel coast were making at least occasional trips to north Cornwall, their cargoes being distributed by ships carrying on coastwise trade. Small boats were needed for landings made on open beaches, but much of the 18th century smuggling seems to have taken place within the main harbours at St Ives, New-quay and Padstow. Every opportunity was also taken to offload goods from West Indies vessels as they headed for Bristol. Rum and sugar were readily available throughout

151

west Cornwall, and it is said that Bristol merchants came to St Ives to buy uncustomed sugar.

One can sympathise with the preventive forces thinly scattered along this great length of wild and often inaccessible coast. Effective control was not generally established until the 1830s, when a full Coastguard service had been organised, and as late as 1844 there were only 79 men in the service between St Ives and Porlock (out of 6,267 in the United Kingdom). At least the exposed coastline meant it was difficult to sink tubs of spirit offshore. The story of specific smuggling episodes here divides naturally into the 18th century pattern, when activities were concentrated around St Ives, Newquay and Padstow, and the situation after 1800 when the free trade increasingly used more difficult landing sites. Finally we leave established fact to consider the legendary figure of Cruel Coppinger, whose alleged activities took place mainly in the remoter northern section of the coast.

St Ives is naturally sheltered from the prevailing winds and had been an important fishing and trading port for centuries before 1700. The local merchants had built up trade relations

St Ives in 1813, from a contemporary print. This important fishing and trading port won an early reputation as a centre for smuggling. Reproduced by kind permission of the Cornish Studies Library, Redruth.

with Ireland and the Mediterranean, and were well placed to intercept West Indies traffic en route to Bristol. Accordingly a Revenue vessel was based at the port by 1698. Shortly after the harbour was improved by Smeaton's new pier, the *Prince Ernst*, described as a sloop in the Custom House service, was 'feloniously and piratically plundered and sunk' by a large smuggling vessel, in May 1772. John Knill was Mayor of the borough in 1767, and Collector of Customs from 1762 to 1782, and it is generally thought that he planned smuggling operations at the George & Dragon Inn. He is believed to have been involved when an unnamed vessel ran aground just east of Carrick Gladden. The crew disappeared inland, and the ship's papers were apparently burnt. When Roger Wearne, the local Customs official, boarded the vessel it was found to be full of china, and other smuggled items. The story is told of how he climbed down the ship's side with his clothes stuffed with samples, only to have these broken when someone (perhaps in the know) hit him a smart blow! It is possible John Knill was the victim of character assassination. He deserves credit for attempts to stop the worst aspects of wrecking. He wrote a pamphlet based on his experience when the Hanover Packet, on her way to Falmouth, was wrecked near St Agnes in 1763. Knill organised 60 men under a special contract to carry out salvage, and claimed that as a result not one of the gold coins recovered from the scene went missing, even though he was not present when they were discovered. This is in sharp contrast to the usual practice here; the local people were liable to burn what they could not carry away! No one is certain why Knill built the steeple on Worvas Hill (though it could have acted as a sea mark) or the significance of the dancing maidens there!

Writing in 1971, Cyril Noall was able to draw on his intimate knowledge of St Ives to explain how, despite a keen watch, 'many ankers were run through the adit, or Cocking's Hole, from Bamaluz Cove to the harbour and hauled up to the old tavern (later called Quay House) standing on Carnsew Rock in Quay Street, through a refuse aperture'.

Apart from what went on at St Ives itself, there were more opportunities right round the bay. Lelant had been a more important port than St Ives before silting prevented this, and 153 smugglers used its shore and are said to have stored goods in the church. Hayle, on the opposite shore, was very important throughout the 18th and early 19th centuries as the outlet for minerals from Redruth and Camborne. There was a flourishing coastwise trade carrying copper to South Wales and bringing back coal and limestone, a useful opportunity for some distribution of contraband. There was copper smelting, an iron foundry, and by 1837 a mineral railway which brought the local ores down to the harbour. Lights from the old Steampacket Hotel and the Britannia Inn (now demolished) guided the smugglers as they approached Hayle harbour.

The whole sandy bay immediately north of here was particularly useful. The goods were landed near Gwithian and carried by packhorse up the valley of the Red River (the colour is from mine waste). Each smuggler managed two horses, the tubs being carried two in front of the rider and two slung each side of the led horse. The convoys proceeded by night via Tuckingmill (east of Camborne) and up the valley southwards past Treskillard and Grillis, dropping off supplies along the way. The much reduced number were then carried up into the Carnmenellis moors to Nine Maidens and Hernis Farm, Stythians. Among the hiding places was a cottage in Carn Brea village near Redruth church, a garden in Stythians Row, Four Lanes and caverns on various local farms. When one tunnel near Mount Wise collapsed under a steam tractor, it took 60 cartloads of material to fill up the hole! These moorland storage pits were equally accessible from Mount's Bay, and the specially constructed one at Wendron has already been described.

The second important centre for 18th century smuggling was Newquay. This long established fishing and trading port was well sheltered by Towan Head, and the 'new quay' dates from 1586. Newquay was to gain added importance after 1830, when a mineral railway was built linking the port to the china clay workings near St Austell. Large schooners came in to transport the clay, and a fleet of pilot gigs met incoming vessels. The importance of the pilchard fishery may be judged from the prominent position of the Huer's House, where a man kept watch for the shoals. It was near this headland that a double cave, known as the Tea Caverns, provided admirable storage. The two caves were separated by a chasm which the smugglers bridged by a plank. According to local tradition this could be turned to precipitate an inquisitive preventive officer into the sea. The inner cave was curved, so that shots could not be fired into it, and the caverns took their name from the commodity most often stored there. The best China tea was widely available at 3/6d a pound in consequence.

Beaches on both sides of Newquay provided other opportunities. To the north was the separate small harbour of Porth. Florey Island here is otherwise known as Black Humphrey's Rock, after a local smuggler and wrecker, and there were numerous caves available for storage. Watergate Bay and Mawgan Porth had obvious advantages, and there is an unhappy tale of wrecking at the latter. An unnamed vessel was driven ashore here in 1754. The crew survived and the ship was in good condition until, as the *Sherborne Mercury* reported 'a parcel of Cornish Barbarians from St Agness, Lower St Columbe etc' arrived on the scene, carried off most of the cargo and burned the ship. A local magistrate had managed to rescue £10,000 worth of raw silk, but was

Newquay Harbour, with the beaches of Porth in the distance. Newquay offered great opportunities for smuggling and admirable storage facilities in the shape of a double cave known as the Tea Caverns.

155

assaulted when he tried to drive off the mob. This magistrate may have been William Rawlings, a wine merchant from St Columb Major seven miles inland. In the 1760s and 1770s he wrote repeatedly to the President of the Board of Trade pointing out how impossible it was for honest businesses to compete against a flood of untaxed wines and spirits. He instanced West Indian rum, available all over Cornwall at 5 shillings a gallon, when he could not offer it at less than 8/6d, and pointed out how the captains and crew of merchantmen took advantage of their opportunities for private trading. he declared that in 1775 it was not uncommon to see 100 horses waiting at Newquay to carry a cargo. The historian Dr Crouch tells an undated story of defiance by smugglers at Newquay Head. Revenue men came on a party who had already stored their cargo in a cave (it is not clear if this was the Tea Caverns). Realising the strength of the opposition, the Revenue men sent for reinforcements, but the smugglers took up positions, armed with cutlasses and sticks. They trained a gun on the cave entrance and dared the preventives to go in. The latter prudently withdrew, and when at last they did gain access, both the smugglers and their goods had disappeared.

There was also a great deal of smuggling on beaches south of Newquay, and storage on both sides of the Gannel. According to the *Western Morning News* there was a smugglers' hole at Tregunnel behind a farmyard and woodrick and others in the farmhouse. At Crantock the Albion Inn had a secret chamber and the belfry was also used. There were popular landing places at Vugga Cove on the east side of West Pentire Point, in Porth (or Polly) Joke and in Holywell Bay. It can be reasonably assumed that there were also landings along Perran Beach, but recorded episodes here date from after 1820.

Padstow was a third centre of smuggling activity, and its seamen already had a dubious reputation before 1700. There were hints of piracy and in 1693 the Collector of Customs was dismissed for taking bribes. The harbour facing onto the sheltered Camel estuary appears at first sight to be the ideal refuge on this difficult coast, but unhappily the Doom Bar at the entrance took a terrible toll of shipping. Nevertheless, Padstow was a long established port for both fishing and general trade. It was to become more prosperous after the harbour approach was improved in 1830. A packet service ran to Bristol and Hayle, and emigrants to the New World left from these quays. Padstow also built ships, and of course its seamen smuggled, despite the presence of a Revenue vessel and a Custom House. William Rawlings recalled how on a moonlit night in 1765 he met 60 horses, each carrying three bags of tea (weighing 56 to 58 lb apiece), which had been landed on a beach two miles west of Padstow and were travelling north into Devon. If he was right about the distance, then the landing could have been in Harlyn or Trevone Bays, but there were other good places between Park and Trevose Heads. In Treyarnon Bay there was said to be a storage place cut into the cliffs, with two entrances (one part way up and the other at the top). Local names like Pepper Cove and Pepper Hole are surely significant, and a Watch House was presently built on Stepper Point at the entrance to Padstow Bay. Porthcothan Beach and the smaller one at Porth Mear next door are partly shielded by the little Trescore Islands; in the event of interference, the smugglers could choose which of the two to use, and either was near the specially constructed vugga already described. It is said that a Revenue officer survived being left to drown at Will's Rock on the north side of Porthcothan Bay.

If the Padstow smugglers had well organised storage on shore, they were equally determined at sea. In August 1791 the *Dolphin* Revenue cutter, based at St Ives, confronted a large smuggling lugger off Padstow. The smugglers fired on the *Dolphin* and demanded that the *Dolphin*'s mate, Mr Osmond, should come on board. He found about 50 men armed for action; there were eight mounted six-pounder guns and more in the hold. Though the *Exeter Flying Post*'s report does not explain what happened after this display of superior strength, no doubt Mr Osmond and the *Dolphin* hastily withdrew. Subsequently a reward of £100 or a free pardon was offered for help towards an arrest, but there is no sign anyone took this up. Popular tradition has preserved another story of defiant smugglers. It is said that a vessel chased the Excise boat *into* Padstow harbour, ran up a triumphant flag, and then sailed off to Newquay.

Stories of smuggling along the whole north Cornish coast

after 1800 come mainly from contemporary newspapers but include some personal recollections. The preventive services were becoming better organised, and in consequence a lot of the action took place along more difficult parts of the coast. South of the Camel river, where the miners provided the main market, there were new opportunities to hide goods on mineral carrying vessels. The first recorded instance of this was at Portreath in 1804. The *Good Intent*, a Barnstaple vessel employed to carry copper ore to South Wales, was caught with a mere six ankers of spirit, a trivial offence, but one the copper company took seriously. They agreed to help in stopping 'this pernicious custom' and went on to advertise the fact in the local press. Porthreath itself dated from around 1760, and was the creation of Francis Basset, patron of Trevithick, who lived at Trehidy nearby. It was built to serve the mines inland, and in 1809 horse-drawn wagons brought the ores along a tramway from Poldice and St Day, and a stationary engine lowered the copper down an incline (which can still be seen) to the harbour. Though there are few actual records of smuggling here, it was an obvious opportunity. It was said that wagons with muffled wheels and a ghostly chariot driven by men dressed as spectres were sometimes seen near Paynter's Lane End, Illogan, some two miles inland from Porthreath. The harbour for the mining district of St Agnes was below the cliffs in Trevaunance Cove. This was inadequately protected by St Agnes Head and five sets of harbour works were washed away over three centuries before it was finally abandoned in the 1930s. A preventive boat was stationed here, and was responsible for seizures in 1823 and 1831.

Troubles continued in all the usual places. In 1805 the *Dart* Revenue cutter seized a vessel and 500 ankers of spirits at Newquay. In 1812 fire destroyed St Ives Custom House and all the records, though there is no indication that foul play was suspected. The boat sitter in charge of the preventive boat discovered a haul of between 200 and 300 casks in 1815. When he and his assistants attempted to seize these, they were violently assaulted by a mob of smugglers, who carried off the goods. Subsequently a reward of £200 was offered for information. St Ives was carefully watched at this point, and we know there was a Riding Officer because his ten-year-old dark brown mare was offered for sale having proved unfit for the service! Further up the coast James Delbridge was fined £75 for 'putting a quantity of smuggled spirits in a cave at Pentire'. (Pentire is the Cornish word for headland, hence the confusing frequency of this placename.)

There were landings near Perranporth. In one amusing incident in 1825 a picnic party from Truro found a tub of brandy when they went to bathe on the beach. This may have been left over from the activities of the local syndicate. According to Captain William Roberts, writing in 1939, his grandfather, who was the general manager of Perranporth's richest copper mine, and a strict Methodist, joined with the vicar and other well-to-do residents to purchase a fast sailing craft called *Cherbourg*. This could outsail the local Revenue vessel and trade directly with its namesake in France. Once the look-out sighted her return, she would be met by small row boats and the cargo landed at Cligga Porth (south-west of Perranporth) or in a double cavern in the cliffs from which the goods were drawn up to the clifftop by derrick, and carried off on muleback. For a time the syndicate prospered, but then a new member betrayed the enterprise. When the *Cherbourg* arrived with what was to be her last cargo, nine coastguards and a naval officer converged on the place. One boatload was landed and concealed before the vessel escaped back to France, pursued by two Revenue cutters. Prudently the syndicate closed operations and a member went to France to sell the vessel and her remaining cargo.

In March 1830 Mr Mortly, a Coastguard officer at Portreath, saw the crew of a cutter using a small boat to land goods on the beach below the formidable cliffs at Hell's Mouth, six miles to the west. That night he and three of his men climbed down the cliffs in darkness at great personal risk (and anyone who looks down these cliffs in broad daylight can only marvel at their courage!) They succeeded in seizing 48 tubs of brandy and 16 of gin (another report speaks of silks and satins), as well as taking the smugglers' boat and two of the crew. Later eight armed smugglers planned to recover their goods by force, and when shots were exchanged, one of the coastguards was hit in the thigh.

By this time the Coastguard service was getting the up- 159

The formidably narrow and winding entrance of Boscastle Harbour. This
print from a painting by J M W Turner shows teams of men on the cliffs at

each side, hauling a vessel into the safety of the harbour. Reproduced by
kind permission of the Cornish Studies Library, Redruth.

perhand. French ships and crewmen were increasingly parti-
cipating in the free trade, since they were not yet subject to
punishment. When in July 1831 five English smugglers and
one Frenchman were caught near St Ives with 99 tubs of
spirit, a chest of tea and a quantity of glass, the Englishmen
were each fined £100, but their French companion escaped
this. Later the same year the French vessel *Elizabeth* came in
with more spirits and glass, apparently aiming for a landing at
Gwithian or Hayle. However, she was warned off, and later
chased and captured. This time the vessel was destroyed in
traditional fashion, with the hull sawn in three pieces. There
were other later seizures involving French crewmen and boats
at Newquay and Morvah in West Penwith, and in 1841 more
tubs were found on Gwithian Beach, but effectively the smuggling era was over here.

North of the Camel Estuary the coast offers little shelter and
few possible landing sites. The three small harbours at Port
Quin, Port Isaac and Port Gaverne served the local fishermen
and later exported slate from Delabole. Boscastle had become
a small port after a pier was built to protect the inner harbour
in 1547, despite the formidable problems of its narrow and
winding entrance. Vessels were either towed in by row boats
or (as in Turner's painting) pulled in by teams of men.
Preventive boats based at Boscastle and Bude were the only
controls along this coast up to the county boundry. The little
harbour built at Hartland Quay in 1566 was in Devon, and
supervised by the Riding Officer at Clovelly. The smuggler
Edward Hockin is said to have operated from Hartland Quay.

The preventive boats based at Boscastle and Bude suffered
mixed fortunes. In November 1820 the Boscastle crew seized
400 or 500 tubs of spirit on the shore at Millook Haven (a
difficult rocky beach used by local fishermen). While they
were guarding their catch, a smuggling cutter appeared and
two boats from her, crewed by armed men, began a battle to
recapture their goods. The exchange of fire continued until the
preventives' ammunition ran out, at which point the smugglers carried off both their contraband and the six-oared
preventive boat. When later the Customs Commissioners
offered £200 for information on the affair, the smuggling cutter
was described as having '16 black ports, 8 of a side, bulwarks

painted with a broad yellow side and a narrow black streak above, red counter with a yellow moulding. . . .' hardly camouflaged! Fifteen months later, when the Boscastle boat was returning to base in a gale, the vessel overturned and all five men on board were drowned.

The Bude preventive boat was involved in a fiasco in 1831, when, having triumphantly boarded and captured a suspect vessel and sailed this back to Bude, she was discovered to hold nothing but salt herrings! However, five years later the crew redeemed themselves by capturing a Fowey vessel with 310 tubs of brandy, which they took into Padstow. It was apparently a chance encounter which led to 100 tubs of spirit, with some tea and tobacco, being seized on the premises of Mrs Hendy of Morwenstow in January 1824. This was believed to have been part of a cargo landed at Marsland Mouth, another difficult and rocky beach right on the county boundary. In the 1840s special warnings were issued to watch for landings at Duckpool (due west of Kilkhampton), as well as Widemouth, Millook and Crackington Havens. Apart from Widemouth Bay, all these last are also difficult beaches among unstable cliffs, not readily accessible by land. Thomas Andrew, the ironmonger at Kilkhampton, was implicated with the notorious Ellery of Probus and two men from Mawgan Porth in another run at this time. Small quantities of spirit were also found concealed under cargoes of coal or lime at Bude.

There remain two well-known stories from the 1850s. Captain James Williams of St Ives landed a cargo of whisky by the old breakwater at St Ives in May 1851. Coastguard Cock, sitting in the parlour of the George & Dragon, was alerted by the noise of wagons outside, but was left tied up as the convoy made off through Hayle towards Redruth. Having freed himself, Cock rode off after the smugglers to the tollhouse at Hayle, where he was carefully misdirected by a bribed toll-keeper. He returned to St Ives and tackled the cabin boy on Williams' boat. The lad had run away to sea from Memel in East Prussia, and convincingly feigned ignorance. This story, known as the Old Worm's Fool (the Old Worm being Williams and the cabin boy his fool) gained wide publicity when Captain Williams wrote a detailed letter of 163 complaint about the detention of his ship, published in the *West Briton* paper. His vessel was then released, but Williams was later tried for smuggling on the evidence of pieces of rope and chain found aboard. The case against him collapsed!

The final story concerns the smack *Wellington* from Plymouth, seen acting suspiciously in Padstow harbour in December 1851. She was chased, but evaded her pursuers long enough for the crew to throw the incriminating tubs overboard. A strong smell of spirits remained when the hatches were opened, and this was confirmed when the bilge water was smelled and (apparently) tasted! It was enough to get each of the crew six months hard labour.

At this stage we leave the factual record to consider the legendary tales of Cruel Coppinger, which haunt the Morwenstow area. They were put together (or fabricated) by the Rev Robert Stephen Hawker in the 1860s, and would not merit serious attention but for a number of intriguing facts and circumstantial evidence. Rev R S Hawker was vicar of Morwenstow from 1834 to his death in 1875. In many respects he was a saintly cleric, poet and scholar, who gave Christian burial to drowned seamen, built and maintained the village school and wrote the *Song of the Western Men*. He was also a thorough-going eccentric, notorious for practical jokes when young. He later became interested in the occult, wrote a book about ghosts and employed as his servant an old smuggler to whom he gave the fictional name of Tristram Pentire. From his servant he no doubt learned much of the truth about local smuggling, which caves were used, where money was left as a bribe for the local Exciseman and so on. According to the stories he told, Cruel Coppinger came from a foreign land and was a Dane. He leapt ashore at Marsland Mouth, the sole survivor of a shipwreck, and rode off on horseback with the local heiress Dinah Hamlyn from Galsham near Hartland. He married her, but then embarked on a ruthless career as head of a gang notorious for wrecking, stealing and smuggling. He owned a vessel called the *Black Prince*. His roistering behaviour and extreme violence eventually brought the threat of retribution, and in the midst of another storm, he jumped onto another ship and disappeared!

164 Now apart from the fact that smuggling and wrecking did

Jamaica Inn on Bodmin Moor was a regular stopping point on the smugglers' route from Cornwall into Devon.

take place close to Morwenstow, there was a privateer called *Black Prince* which harried the area until destroyed by Harry Carter. There was also a Daniel Herbert Coppinger who married Ann (not Dinah) Hamlyn of Galsham Farm at Hartland in August 1793. The marriage certificate claims he was in the Royal Navy, though no record confirms this. Scratched into a window pane with his name is the statement that he was shipwrecked on 23rd December 1792, and kindly received by William Arthur, a local farmer. So D H Coppinger is the obvious candidate for the Cruel Coppinger legend, but his name does not feature in the Custom House records, nor does his subsequent life suggest he was either cruel or successful. He went bankrupt in 1802, spent a period in gaol and then lived in Barnstaple on an allowance from his wife.

It is another possibility which has intrigued investigators from Rev Baring-Gould to Hippisley-Coxe, and the latter's work has recently added to our knowledge. John Copinger (with one 'p') was an extremely successful smugglers' merchant operating from Roscoff in the late 18th century. He came from Ireland, where his forebears had lived for centur-

165

ies, but the family may originally have come from Denmark. John Copinger first moved from Ireland to Cornwall, and then went to Roscoff. His success may be judged from the tax he paid in 1785, when Copinger, Clancie and Company was assessed at £260, compared with the Maccullochs, who paid £48, and Diot & Co taxed at £24. Following the French Revolution, rich merchants were classed with aristocrats and suffered confiscation of their assets, imprisonment and the threat of execution. John Copinger evidently got out in time and settled in Cornwall, according to circumstantial evidence at Trewhiddle, just south-west of St Austell. It is thought he may have been actively involved in smuggling, using a vessel based at Mevagissey. In any case Trewhiddle is a mere 2½ miles from the smuggling beach at Porthpean. Meanwhile William Clancie, the Maccullochs and Diot were caught and imprisoned in Brittany, where Harry Carter came to know them well, but he made no reference to a Copinger. According to Hippisley-Coxe, John Copinger's eldest son, James George, went over to France during the Revolution to get his younger brother and sister out. He too was arrested, but evidently survived, and several of John Copinger's grandchildren were later living in France. But why is there no record of John Copinger at Trewhiddle, and why did Harry Carter never mention his name, despite being the intimate friend of his business associate William Clancie? The Rev Baring-Gould states categorically that John Copinger was spying for England while in Roscoff, and hence carefully protected by the authorities. His two daughters made eminently respectable marriages, and two sons served in the Navy. He cannot, of course, be equated with Cruel Coppinger, but he could have been involved in smuggling while at Trewhiddle. If that were so, Harry Carter would have avoided all reference to his activities in the same way as he carefully protected his own brothers, when writing his autobiography. One final twist to the story: John Copinger's ancestors, living at Carbery in Ireland, included some violent and vicious individuals. At least three were outlawed for High Treason. Did the real John Copinger draw on their behaviour when manufacturing Cruel Coppinger to distract attention from his own many-sided business interests?

166

PLACES TO VISIT

St Ives

Of all the Cornish fishing settlements St Ives is perhaps the most fascinating. Explore the streets of the old core on foot! The village grew up on the narrow isthmus which linked the mainland to the low hill offshore known as The Island or St Ives Head. The maze of lower streets form Downalong, the fishermen's quarter, those in Upalong above were inhabited by miners working in the Stennack area. Other interesting names include The Digey (fishermen's cottages with outside staircases) Rope Walk and Teetotal Street (a legacy of Wesley's visits). Above the harbour, with Smeaton's pier of 1767, stands the Old Custom House (next door to Woolworth's), and the George & Dragon Inn is said to be where the smugglers planned their activities. Even before Turner's visit the qualities of light and the quaint buildings had attracted a colony of artists and craftsmen here. Customs Collector Knill's strange monument on a hilltop can be reached from A3074 behind Carbis Bay. The next occasions when ten virgins and two widows dance round the base will be 25th July 1991 and 1996!

Gwithian, Godrevy and Hell's Mouth

(Carpark on Gwithian Beach at SW 579413 approached from B3301, ½ mile south of village.) Landings took place on the beach between here and Red River to the north. (Alternative carpark at Godrevy Point, SW 581431, reached along rough track from bridge over Red River.) There are excellent views of the whole bay and Godrevy Lighthouse which was the inspiration for Virginia Woolf's *To The Lighthouse*. The B3301 comes close to the clifftop at Hell's Mouth, and there is roadside parking. Portreath Harbour, further east, was built in 1760 and is an interesting site for industrial archaeology. Trehidy nearby is the former home of Francis Basset, patron of Trevithick. Ralph's Cupboard, on the cliffs, is said to be a hiding place for contraband.

167

SMUGGLING IN DEVON AND CORNWALL

Perranporth

Perranporth has a tremendous sandy beach to the north and very fine cliffs and stacks to the south-west. To see the sort of places where contraband was carried up by primitive derricks, follow the coast path up towards Cligga Head (keeping a careful eye on disused mine shafts!) Pass the Youth Hostel on Droskyn Point, and shortly beyond look over the cliff to see a shaft which comes up to a lower platform, with obvious roadways etc. There is a fine cliff walk the whole way to Trevaunance Cove, the former port for St Agnes and interesting industrial archaeology all round St Agnes.

Crantock, West Pentire and Porth Joke

(Carpark at West Pentire Farm SW 776607.) Follow the footpath between hedges towards the north side of the headland, turning down towards the coast at the first gate, but avoiding the path over the stile leading back to the beach. Vugga Cove (SW 775610) is below among rocks, a great trench cut by the sea in upturned slates. The cave itself (or Vugga) has fallen in. Continue round towards Pentire Head along the lower cliff path, passing a hole into a collapsed cave, and so round to Porth or Polly Joke – the perfect small smuggling beach! One hiding place was at Treago Watermill (now holiday cottages) just up the valley and near the National Trust carpark. From Porth Joke the coast path leads round to Holywell Beach, another landing site. The holy well is in a cave on the north side of this bay. In Crantock village there were hiding places in the Old Albion Inn and inside a white-washed cottage opposite Crantock village well at the corner of Beach Road.

Newquay and Porth

Though Newquay has developed greatly since 1700, there is still much of interest among the fine cliffs and beaches. Apart from the harbour, an excellent clifftop walk leads out to Towan Head, passing the strange Huer's Hut, now thought to have been a 14th century hermitage and light for shipping, but later where the Huer kept watch for the pilchard shoals. From here to Towan Head the cliff path runs beside the bay called the Gazzle; various caves in these cliffs include the smugglers' Tea Caverns. There are more smugglers' caves at the east end of Newquay in the bay called Lusty Glaze, and round the headland towards Porth are Wine Cave and The Great Cupboard. Porth Beach was also used, and there were more large caverns below the coast path out to Trevelgue Head (the path starts from B3276 beside the Pitch and Putt course). The huge Banqueting Hall cave, once used for concerts but blown up as unsafe in 1987, was just south of this path, close to the bridge onto Trevelgue Head and its important Bronze and Iron Age settlement site. The view from here is magnificent and includes smuggler Black Humphrey's Rock (or Florey Island) and Whipsiderry Beach, a name thought to refer to the derricks used to bring up goods from the shore.

Porthcothan Beach
(Carpark beside B3276 at Porthcothan.) Follow the coast path south-west and turn down to the beach just beyond the last house to the narrow straight-sided bay with small caves, stacks etc. in dark slate cliffs – excellent for a picnic or a swim today, or a landing 200 years ago! Follow the coast path round the headland to the south-west, past holes into the caves below, to reach Porth Mear, a cove fringed by rocks and partly shielded by Trescore Islands. A valley leads inland to Trevemedar. Goods could be landed on either beach and then rolled or carried towards secret passages and the Vugga store. The latter (as described on page 150) is on private land. The coast path continues on National Trust land round Park Head, with excellent views. The National Trust has a useful leaflet on the area.

Padstow
Use the main carpark and explore Padstow on foot with its fine core of old slate-hung buildings. On North Quay is a 15th century Merchants' Guild House and on South Quay is 16th century Raleigh's Court House where his agents collected dues when he was Lord Warden of the Stanneries. The church is dedicated to the 6th century Irish St Petroc. On May 1st every year hobby horse ceremonies are held. Note that Port Isaac is the most interesting of various small fishing and smuggling ports north of the Camel estuary. There is   169

some parking and turning space on the beach beside the harbour, but do not attempt this lightly!

Millook Haven and neighbouring beaches
Crackington Haven and Widemouth Bay are easier to reach, were used for landings and show similar features, but Millook was the setting for the episode in 1820. The approach roads are very steep and narrow and there is little space to park. Unstable cliffs with contorted strata rise above a stony beach which must always have been difficult, but note the remains of a capstan. There is a good carpark and view from the summit between Millook Haven and Widemouth Bay at SS 187006.

Duckpool, Coombe Valley and Morwenstow
(Near Cleave Camp Satellite Station.) Approach Coombe Valley from A39, ½ mile south of Kilkhampton, following signs. Pass Stowe Barton, a fortified 17th century farmhouse, descend steeply to cross a stream and turn left down to the beach at Duckpool and a National Trust carpark; this is a stony beach among unstable cliffs, but one the smugglers used. Continue north past the satellite station for 2½ miles to reach Morwenstow. Note the Old Bush Inn, St Morwenna's church with graves of shipwrecked sailors, Hawker's vicarage (with chimneys representing churches where he served). Hawker's hut is on the clifftop, a short walk across fields and on National Trust land. Note that the shingly beach at Marsland Mouth is only accessible on foot, and that Welcombe Mouth is reached only down a very rough lane.

10

The North Devon Coast from Hartland Point to County Gate

East of Hartland Point one enters the Bristol Channel. The full story of what took place along the entire coastline during the main smuggling period has already been told in the companion volume in this series (*Smuggling in the Bristol Channel 1700–1850*, by Graham Smith). However, despite some inevitable duplication, it is appropriate to include here the main developments within north Devon. Because much of this coast was remote and undeveloped throughout the 18th century, authentic details of what took place are disappointingly meagre, and I am indebted to Graham Smith's research for an account of many smuggling episodes. The best records come from the correspondence of the Collectors of Customs at the ports of Ilfracombe, Barnstaple and Bideford, who were responsible for the tiny harbours at Hartland, Clovelly, Appledore, Instow, Heddon's Mouth and Lynmouth in addition to the three main ports. After 1790 several West Country papers also reported smuggling episodes. For the rest, folk memory has kept alive many stories of people and places involved in the trade, which it is now impossible to authenticate.

The north Devon coast is celebrated for the magnificence of its scenery. From the weather-beaten and contorted rocks of Hartland Point the coast turns eastwards, following the natural grain of the rocks and countryside. Cliffs rise behind unwelcoming rocky shorelines, an almost unbroken rampart some 400 ft high in many places. Characteristically these cliffs steepen towards the bottom, a hogsback shape which adds to the difficulty of reaching the shore below, and the less exposed 171

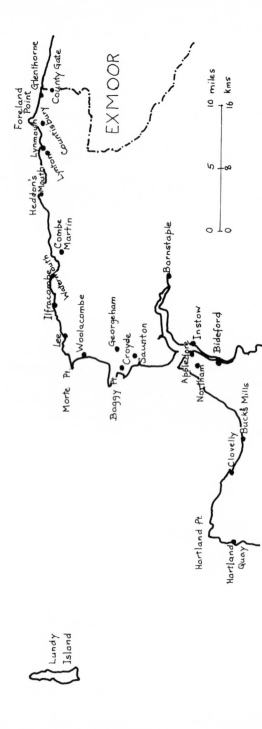

Places associated with the smuggling trade in north Devon.

stretches are thickly wooded. For small vessels the only shelter was in remote Shipload Bay, at Clovelly or Buck's Mills nearby.

Then at Westward Ho! there is a complete change; the coast turns north again, and the cliffs fall away to be replaced by huge expanses of sand at Braunton and Northam Burrows. Here the joint waters of the Taw and Torridge rivers flow out into Bideford Bay over a bar. For many centuries ships from the ancient seaports of Barnstaple, Bideford and Appledore left this protected estuary to trade with Ireland, France, Portugal, Spain and the American Colonies, and fishing fleets went annually to the Grand Banks off Newfoundland. Once past the great range of sand dunes at Saunton, however, the cliffs reappear, first with the resistant sandstones and grits of Baggy Point, and then with the sharper slates of Morte Point, the graveyard of so many ships over the centuries. Thereafter the coast runs eastwards to the county boundary and beyond. Here the cliffs rise in places to over 1,000 ft along the northern edge of Exmoor, and the fretted sequence of coves and headlands forms some of the most magnificent scenery in the country. Much of Exmoor is still remote and almost unpopulated; in past centuries this was a lawless backwater celebrated in the story of *Lorna Doone*. Small landing places developed only where deeply cut valleys led down to rocky bays. Ilfracombe and Lynmouth are the only harbours of any size, though Lee Bay to the west, Samson's and Watermouth Bays east of Ilfracombe, Heddon's Mouth and Countisbury Cove below Exmoor were all patronised by the free traders.

At first sight this coast offered little to the smugglers, indeed any vessel entering these waters after successfully evading a Revenue Cutter would have found it easier to land goods on the sheltered beaches of Gower or Swansea bay, and more profitable too, thanks to the potential market among the Welsh miners. On the other hand, the very harshness of the Devon coast meant that much of it was left virtually unwatched, at least during the 18th century. All the Bristol Channel ports were close enough to have developed a thriving cross channel and coastwise trade. In particular Welsh limestone, coal and culm (soft powdery coal) were regularly shipped to make the lime needed to sweeten acid moorland soils, 173 in the limekilns which are still a feature of the north Devon coast. What better cargo to mask a speculative clutch of brandy kegs? Then there was the passing traffic on its way to the thriving port of Bristol. Bristol pilots, both official and otherwise, used Ilfracombe as their base while awaiting the arrival of vessels from the American Colonies and West Indies, and like their counterparts in the Scillies and west Cornwall who met incoming East Indiamen, made good use of their opportunities. In any case all the Bristol Channel ports traded with Ireland, where Customs controls were notoriously lax, and had access to the specialised suppliers of Rush. On balance therefore, although there were none of the large clandestine landings met by hundreds of horsemen, a steady stream of contraband came ashore in smaller quantities.

The Board of Customs was also extensively swindled through documentation frauds in the rival ports of Barnstaple and Bideford, and their smaller quays at Appledore and Instow, where trade in the 18th century was dominated by the import of tobacco. Typically this came in legally and Custom dues were paid, before it was shipped out again, ostensibly to a foreign country, so that the duty could be reclaimed, before the tobacco filtered back into England by other means. If the merchants outwitted the Revenue by drawback of duty, the ships' crews used less subtle means. As they neared port the men threw carefully wrapped parcels overboard, to be collected by friends in small boats or washed ashore on the tide. Such quantities of tobacco came in near Instow (whether in good condition or damp and musty) that in 1735 there was a complaint about damage done to the field where contraband was regularly destroyed by burning. However, the owner of the field agreed this could continue, providing that he might have the ashes! As Lords of the Manor, the Luttrell family were also keenly interested in this flotsam and jetsam!

Around 1700 Barnstaple and Bideford were at the height of their prosperity, with old established trading links to Ireland, France, Portugal, Spain, the West Indies and American Colonies. Bideford had a reputation for its shipbuilding, and was second only to London for the import of tobacco. Barnstaple was the older settlement, and had achieved borough status before the Norman Conquest. During the Middle Ages it imported Irish wool for its cloth industry, and the town was sufficiently wealthy to equip and send five vessels to fight the Armada. Unfortunately, after 1700 the Taw estuary began to silt up, and Barnstaple lost trade to its neighbour Bideford. Appledore had also taken part in the Irish wool trade, and has maintained its maritime links and shipbuilding to this day. In the 18th century it also imported tobacco and was often the centre of the struggle against smuggling. Here I must declare an interest: among my forebears are sea-captains from Appledore who lie buried in Northam churchyard beneath the tower which was a sea mark for so long. At the very least they must have known what was going on!

Bideford developed later. In Norman times King William II granted the manor to Sir Richard de Grenville, and a market and fair were established here in the 13th century. It was another Grenville who built the marvellous 15th century bridge of 24 arches, and yet another Sir Richard Grenville who obtained the town's charter from Elizabeth I in 1573, helped to colonise Virginia and Carolina, and in his famous ship the *Revenge* fought the Spaniards in the Azores. Like other great Devon seamen of the period, he traded overseas with cheerful disregard for Customs regulations, so it is hardly surprising that from among the wealthy merchants of Bideford, accustomed to venturing their capital on projects both legal and otherwise, there came Thomas Benson MP, Sheriff of Devon and smuggler extraordinary, who was to mastermind operations from Lundy.

The name Lundy means island of puffins, and is Norse – an indication of its strategic value to seagoing marauders. A mere half a mile wide and some three miles from north to south, it lies 12 miles north-west of Hartland Point. Formed of granite and rising to over 400 ft, it is flanked on all sides by cliffs and a rocky shore. Only at the extreme south-east tip is there a sheltered cove where landings are possible, and this in turn is overlooked by defences erected over the centuries. Any determined occupier of this fortified bastion could command the shipping lane to Bristol itself, and the island lay outside the control of any port in 1700. For centuries it had been used as a hideout by pirates, both Westcountrymen like Robert Hickes of Saltash and John Peers of Padstow, and other adventurers 175 from France, Spain or Algeria. Things were quieter by the early 18th century, when Robert Scores was a tenant farmer on the island, but the Customs Collectors at the nearest ports were fully aware of the quantities of contraband being stored or transshipped here. Indeed, in 1723 men from Barnstaple rowed out in their preventive boat to seize a large consignment of tobacco and spirits on Lundy.

The number of men who could be called on for preventive work at this time was pathetically small. For example there were only four unarmed men to supervise the trade of the port of Ilfracombe. Probably the most useful defence against smuggling was the Customs smack based there before 1700, responsible for patrolling the Bristol Channel. Picture the difficulties of a single Riding Officer responsible for a ten mile stretch of this rugged coastline, and based among communities dedi-

Ilfracombe in 1774, a harbour of refuge along an otherwise dangerous and inhospitable coast. This contemporary engraving shows shipping in the sheltered harbour, and the Welsh coast in the distance. Reproduced by kind permission of West Country Studies Library, Exeter.

176

cated to evading all controls. The temptation to succumb to bribery, or at least to make a deal with the smugglers for part of a haul must have been almost overwhelming. In 1804 the Collector at Barnstaple felt compelled to draw attention to 'the total incompetency of John Berry, Riding Officer of Clovelly, who was appointed to guard the coast from thence to Bude. He is exceedingly infirm being upwards of 70 years old and we understand that he has not been on horseback for 20 years past'!

Turning now to known smuggling episodes, there were almost no seizures of goods during the early 18th century, from which one must conclude that the free trade went on everywhere without significant interference. The 1740s saw major expansion of smuggling in many parts of Britain. Barnstaple was involved in the illegal export of wheat, and in April 1746 there was a riot, and the Customs warehouse was broken into and stored wheat taken. But it was Thomas Benson's activities which focused attention on the extent of the illicit trade in north Devon. In 1743 Benson inherited Knapp House, Northam, more than a dozen vessels and a family business built up on trade with the American Colonies, France and Portugal. His total assets were said to be worth £40,000 – a huge sum at that time. His ship the *Benson Galley* (with 20 guns) was then the only licensed privateer in north Devon, but other vessels in his fleet also attacked foreign shipping. He also built a new quay at Appledore. By 1748 he was Sheriff of Devon and Member of Parliament for Barnstaple, and used his position to obtain a contract to ship convicts to the American Colonies (at £20 per head) and then return with tobacco. One might have thought these perfectly legal activities would have satisfied him, but in 1748 he went on to acquire the lease of Lundy and embark on grander schemes. He shipped the convicts no further than Lundy and set them to work fortifying his island stronghold and providing storage there.

At this stage the Collector at Barnstaple reported to his superiors 'The smugling trade on this coast is again begun, a vessell or two having very lately . . . run brandy, claret etc in Lundy Road in our bay and as a general peace is expected [after the War of the Austrian Succession] we are very appre- 177

The quay at Appledore, built by Thomas Benson in 1745. This thriving port has a strong maritime past and smuggling tradition and it is from here that Benson planned many of his operations.

hensive that this pernicious trade of smugling will again be carryed on with impunity unless a smack is ordered to prevent it and stationed . . . at Appledore'. Three years later the Collector sought advice; Thomas Benson was asking for tobacco and provisions to be sent out to Lundy and he did not know how to respond. Little positive action seems to have been taken; in 1752 the Board of Customs merely restated the position: 'a new trade is carried on at the island of Lundy and that many ships bound outwards from Barnstaple Bay unload there and that cargoes are afterwards returned to that country in other vessels. That a platform with guns is erected & shot fired to bring ships too for to give an account who and what they are, but the men in them are not suffered to land. . .'

In the end the Board in London issued writs against Benson for repayment of over £8,300 in duty on tobacco they believed had been smuggled back to the mainland. Benson was further tried before the House of Lords for failing to fulfill his contract to ship convicts to Virginia. (Eight of the convicts had escaped and come ashore at Hartland Quay.) In what must surely have been an act of folly, in July 1752 he sailed his laden ship *Nightingale* to Lundy (having heavily insured both vessel and cargo), unloaded the cargo on Lundy and then sailed westwards, before firing and scuttling the empty vessel. He and the crew then managed to come ashore near Clovelly, and Benson went on to submit a fraudulent insurance claim. But presently a seaman talked, the game was up, and Benson was lucky to escape to Portugal, while the master of the *Nightingale* was convicted and executed. Despite attempts to have Benson extradited, he continued trading in Portugal and died in his bed in 1771.

There are other records of smuggling during these years. In 1747 a large Irish wherry was observed unloading a cargo of brandy, tobacco and soap off Braunton Burrows. This huge expanse of sand dunes offered the maximum opportunities for concealment, so it is hardly surprising that Joseph Mellor, the local Riding Officer, secured a mere three casks. However, the naval vessel *Despatch* was based at Appledore for a time in the 1750s to help the Barnstaple Collector. In 1752 men from the *Despatch* found pieces of linen and lawn with 13 ankers of rum concealed beneath a cargo of culm brought in from Neath. Four years later, when a naval vessel was sailing near Porlock in Somerset, an Irish wherry was spotted acting suspiciously at Gore Point below Culbone, which was within the Ilfracombe collection area. When the naval ship fired a warning shot the Irish wherry fled precipitately, but naval seamen found only small amounts of damaged tea and brandy kegs in a search on shore. There were also instances of petty smuggling on vessels engaged in coastwise trade: six tubs of spirit under a cargo of fish; two ankers of brandy, some wine and six small bales of tobacco under coal brought from Swansea to Appledore, for example. The master of the collier admitted that he had called at Lundy on his way over, and confirmed that the island remained an entrepot for contraband.

It is noticeable that during the 1750s and 1760s much of the preventive activity was concentrated around Appledore. The Board in London sent instructions to the Tidesurveyor there to let them know the names and habitations of the offenders. In June 1763 Mr George Wackrill, the Landwaiter at Instow on the opposite shore, received a curt instruction: 'We direct

179

you to acquaint us of the reasons (if you can find any) why you had not been at Instow Key last night with your key of the King's Warehouse in order to receive two hogsheads of brandy and lodge them under your joynt care and we also desire to know how your lock came to be unlocked & when you visited the warehouse last & also how long a time you have been absent from Instow key, to all which questions we expect a downright answer in writing by toMorrow or Tuesday Morng at farthest. . .' Meanwhile, jettisoned packets of tobacco continued to come ashore, and there were reports that seamen were dropping parcels of paper and other goods overboard, to be collected by a flotilla of small boats.

The 1780s saw a resurgence of smuggling everywhere in the country. Lundy was once again the centre of operations, but even the smallest islands in the Bristol Channel acted as storage depots or smugglers' headquarters. Barry island was the unlikely setting from which Thomas Knight carried on his smuggling empire until 1785, when he is believed to have moved to Lundy. Both Steepholm and Flatholm off Weston-super-Mare are known to have been used as bases during these years. The fortifications on Lundy had been greatly strengthened with the addition of a long list of guns, weapons and ammunition – enough, according to the Barnstaple Collector, to sustain a long siege! These activities had alerted Customs officials on the South Wales coast. Though they regarded Lundy as the main threat, they believed that there was an increase in contacts with the specialised suppliers of contraband in both Ireland and France, and reported that armed vessels from the Channel Islands and smaller Cornish craft were bringing brandy, gin and salt to Barry Island, Sully and Aberthaw on the Welsh coast. The Swansea Collector sent two boats to search Lundy, and his men found 128 ankers of brandy and four bags of Bohea tea (a relatively small haul considering the reputation of the place!)

It was while Thomas Knight was operating from Lundy in 1786 that an Irish wherry landed spirits and tobacco on the shore at Heddon's Mouth – a tiny landing place at the foot of a deep valley some 3½ miles west of Lynmouth. (A limekiln here is almost the only evidence of the coastwise trade which once came to this remote spot.) The vessel was believed to have belonged to Knight, but both it and the landing party escaped, leaving the preventive men with 20 ankers of spirits and 13 bales of tobacco. Another notorious smuggler, William Arthur, who came from Pennard in Gower, had his vessel regularly but unsuccessfully searched as it returned from meeting shipping in the Bristol Channel, and finally in 1782 gin and six bags of tea were found on board, enough for the vessel to be seized and sawn in three as the law directed.

The sand dunes of Northam Burrows were regularly and fruitlessly searched by men based at Appledore, but then in 1782 the Revenue cutter *Scorpion* seized 50 ankers of brandy, 150 lb of tobacco and four bags of tea on the beach there. The goods had been landed from a Cornish smack which traded regularly between north Cornwall and Bristol. At Instow, where the Tidewaiter also spent frustrating hours searching the sands, 210 casks of spirits and a quantity of tobacco were found in 1783, close to Instow Quay. In the event this led to arguments over prize money because the seizure took place close to the boundary between the two collection areas.

At this time more patrols by Revenue vessels were leading to successful seizures, but the Revenue Cutter *Fox*, stationed at Ilfracombe from 1787 to 1790 was too small to be effective. The Excise Cutter *Ferret*, based at Milford Haven but able to patrol the north Devon coast, was more successful, much of the activity taking place around Ilfracombe. In 1789 the *Ferret* caught the *Success* of Padstow carrying 1,084 lb of tobacco and 280 lb of snuff; unusually this was packed in waterproof bladders and ready to be sunk offshore. There were smaller catches two years later: 500 lb of tobacco in a collier from Cardiff; gin and brandy on a smack from Mevagissey, and 250 lb of tobacco in an open pilot gig, the goods only just purchased from an outward-bound Spanish vessel.

The pillaging of wrecks was a regular activity on these coasts. When in 1738 the *Bedra* from Ireland came ashore on Saunton Sands with a cargo of soap and candles, the local population disposed of everything. However, in January 1791 when the *Abeona* was driven on Northam Burrows, the preventivemen were quicker on the scene. The *Abeona* was a large new armed smuggling cutter from Fowey. Her master, Christopher Parnell, had a crew of 22 and the vessel had fittings for 181

16 six-pounder guns (these had been thrown overboard). Her cargo was judged to be worth £5,000 and consisted of 700 ankers of spirits, tea, tobacco and dry goods, silk, china and playing cards. This is an interesting case, not only because it shows how Fowey smugglers shipped goods to north Devon, but also because the *Abeona* and her cargo were so much more valuable than most seizures on this coast. That the smuggling syndicates of Fowey were not deterred by this loss is clear from the capture of several more of their vessels some 15 years later. In May 1799 the smuggling cutter *Hope* was wrecked in Watermouth Bay, a small but sheltered cove just east of Ilfracombe. The vessel had already landed 96 tubs of brandy at Heddon's Mouth, and was about to land a further 80 when she hit the rocks and sank with all hands.

Throughout this period the Collectors at Barnstaple, Bideford and Ilfracombe kept up their appeals for more men and ships to hold the smuggling trade in check. The *Racer*, a small additional Revenue Cutter, was sent to patrol the coasts from Ilfracombe to Chepstow, and in 1800 the naval cutter *Dover* gave further help by seizing the *Endeavour* of Bideford, caught hovering off the aptly-named Brandy Cove just west of Ilfracombe. Her cargo was a valuable one – 1,076 gallons of brandy, 500 of gin and 225 of rum, as well as 5 cwt of salt. But the Ilfracombe Collector had no doubts about the extent of the problem. He specified Lee and Samson's Bays, Heddon's Mouth, Lynmouth and Countisbury Cove as the worst places, and his colleague at Barnstaple added Clovelly to the list. The seizures and discoveries continued. In 1802 an Excise officer made the unusual find of a 96 gallon cask of rum in an outhouse at Watermouth which was perhaps intended as a bribe. Then in 1805 the Revenue Cutter *Shark* made a series of substantial seizures, two of which were large vessels from Fowey. In March the *Dart* lugger was caught off Clovelly, laden with spirits, tobacco and pepper from Guernsey. In June the *Shark* brought into Barnstaple what was described as a beautiful new cutter, the *Ida* of Fowey, with 700 large ankers of brandy and gin. The *Ida* had been caught in the Irish Channel after a chase lasting 16 hours, and the papers reported that this was the fourth important seizure by the *Shark*
in six months. Two years later the Excise cutter *Resolution*

caught yet another large Fowey vessel, the *Mary Ann*, when she ran aground near Lynmouth, having already landed 600 ankers of brandy. William Lilburn, Commander of the *Resolution*, took the vessel into Ilfracombe, but all the brandy had vanished by the time he got back to Lynmouth, and he was convinced the local Riding Officer was in collusion with the smugglers.

Twice in 1817 vessels came into Ilfracombe for shelter or urgent repairs, but then unloaded part of their cargo. In the case of the Portuguese vessel *Felix Restoracion* it was merely noted that the ship rode much higher in the water by the time she left, but Revenue Officers kept careful watch on the *Mary Jane*, en route to Bristol from the West Indies, and were able to pounce when 300 gallons of rum, 500 gallons of wine and 1,000 lb of tobacco were taken ashore in the early hours of the morning.

Two quite different aspects of smuggling were reported in the press at this time. The *Sherborne Mercury* warned: 'the public are cautioned against some persons who have defrauded several people in Swansea, Ilfracombe, Bideford and Minehead by selling anker casks of water under the pretence of its being smuggled spirits'. Apparently each had inside a small vessel containing good quality spirits which customers could sample – a neat touch! The *Royal Cornwall Gazette* reported in 1819 that Mr Brown, fish salter of Clovelly, was convicted in the Court of Exchequer for 'misapplying salt, received by him for curing fish, to some other purpose, and thereby defrauding the Revenue'. He was fined £154.14 shillings. Incidentally, the last recorded seizure of a vessel at Clovelly was in April 1825, when the 37 ton *Hope* was arrested.

The years from 1790 to 1810 mark a watershed in the smuggling annals of north Devon. Unmistakably the preventive forces were gaining the upper hand, and the merchants of Fowey had particular cause to reconsider their activities. Lundy had now been neutralised and reports in the West Country press show that public attitudes were changing. The free traders fell back on small scale operations and on greater emphasis on concealment. The many caves, sand dunes and areas of woodland meant there was little need for elaborate artificial hiding places on shore, but rough seas and a large

183

tidal range made it difficult to sink rafts of tubs offshore as was common elsewhere. The records show that more of the ventures were now being attempted along the north coast of Exmoor at Countisbury Cove or on the county boundary. We can sympathise with the smugglers' lookout, stationed on Foreland Point, Countisbury, who in old age told the Rev W H Thornton how cold it was lying there, waiting to show the triangle of three lights rigged on the back of his donkey to the vessel below as it approached what is now Glenthorne House. (There is a useful cellar at the gatekeeper's cottage at County Gate above Glenthorne Beach.) No doubt it was partly because more runs were taking place below Exmoor that the first Coastguard Station on this coast was established at Duty Point, Lee Bay (west of Lynmouth, and not to be confused with the larger Lee Bay west of Ilfracombe, where a Riding Officer was already stationed.) In 1827 there was another seizure at Heddon's Mouth. The contraband, a total of 262 tubs, had been hidden on a Trentishoe farm, and the farmer, John Hoyle, escaped capture. A determined but unsuccessful attempt was made to retrieve the tubs as these were carted away. Five years later the Lynmouth Riding Officer, Michael Sullivan, seized three horses with 64 tubs of spirit on Countisbury Common. According to the two farm labourers involved, the goods had been brought ashore in Countisbury Cove from a gentleman's yacht. Apparently the landing had been interrupted, and the yacht went on to Appledore to unload a further 24 tubs. Then in January 1835, in a reversal of the usual pattern, the Porlock vessel *Prudence & Jane* was caught near Fowey, presumably on the way to buy supplies.

At this stage all large scale smuggling had ceased, although around 1844 some increase in minor ventures was reported: 103 tubs of spirit seized at Bideford; and at Barnstaple 55 bales of tobacco and stalks and 108 tubs of brandy. It seems that petty smuggling had become more prevalent in Somerset, where the Collector at Bridgwater commented that 'no part of the coast offers better chances because of lack of patrols'. Certainly the tradition lived on. Sometime in the 1850s Samuel Bray, the farmer at Woodhead Farm near Beer in east Devon, drove a wagon to a place on the north coast of Devon, where he picked up a load of brandy kegs. He got back, after a round trip of some 130 miles, only to be caught at the toll gate on Trow Hill (the present A3052). Samuel Bray went to prison, while his frustrated customers burned the tollkeeper's effigy in disgust – a story which takes this survey of smuggling on the coast of Devon and Cornwall full circle, for we are back once more in Rattenbury country!

PLACES TO VISIT

Clovelly
This celebrated tourist spot and historic fishing village has been carefully preserved by the Hamlyn family, Lords of the Manor at Clovelly Court since 1738. Sir James Hamlyn constructed the Hobby Drive, now a toll road and the best approach; (off A39 from Hobby Lodge at SS 336233). Caves along the drive are said to have been used for storage. There is parking, a picnic area and newly-built Clovelly Centre just above the village. Picturesque houses line the steep cobbled descent (used by donkeys) to the 16th century quay where Benson came ashore, and the Red Lion, reputed to be a smuggling inn. Local boat trips are available. There is a Land Rover service for those wishing to avoid the steep ascent back. Buck's Mills, further east, is a smaller, quieter hamlet with a smuggler's cottage and impressive lime kiln. (Approach off A39 at Buck's Cross SS 348228.)

Appledore
From the A39 just west of the new bridge over the river Torridge, turn north (A386), passing Knapp House, now a holiday activity centre, but once Thomas Benson's home. Continue to the waterfront and quay at Appledore. There is a passenger ferry to Instow Quay (where George Wackrill failed to keep an eye on the warehouse!) The museum and historic streets are just behind the quay. The Old Custom House stands on the seafront at the north end with a commanding view of vessels sailing over Bideford Bar; also Coastguard cottages and a lifeboat station. Northam Burrows Country Park (approached past Northam church) gives an idea of the sands and dunes where much contraband came ashore. A pebble ridge defines the coastline here.

185

Croyde and Woolacombe Bays

Today's excellent sands and surfing beaches were once patronised by smugglers. For the best walk use the carpark at the north end of Croyde Bay (SS 436396) and follow the coast path round Baggy Point with dramatic views of Saunton sands and across to Appledore from the headland of steeply inclined ripple-marked rocks. The area is good for birdwatching. There are thatched and stone cottages in Croyde village and a smuggling inn at Georgeham.

Ilfracombe and Lee

Ilfracombe harbour has changed little since the smuggling epoch, though the town developed greatly as a tourist resort in Victorian times. Today visitors can enjoy the local museum and bathing beaches. Torrs Walk to the west continues along the coast path to Lee village (passing Brandy Cove and Smuggler's Leap). (Alternative route to Lee by car from B3231.) This attractive village in a narrow valley has a small beach among slate cliffs, Smuggler's Cottage and a fine old inn. To the east of Ilfracombe, Samson's Bay, Watermouth Bay and Combe Martin Bay were all used for landings. Chambercombe Manor, to the south-east, is the ancient manor house of Ilfracombe with a priest's hole and haunted room and reputed to have had a tunnel. (Open daily except Saturdays, main season.)

Lundy Island

There are regular sailings from Bideford Quay throughout the year, and from Ilfracombe during the summer season only. Check details from Tourist Information Centres at Bideford (Tel 0237-477676) or Ilfracombe (0271-863001). Advance booking is essential in high season. Lundy belongs to the Landmark Trust.

Heddon's Mouth

The carpark at Hunter's Inn (SS 656482) is approached down steep narrow roads from A39. Signed footpaths lead down both sides of the valley floor through oak woods to the tiny beach and recently restored limekiln where the contraband came ashore. Alternatively walk from Hunter's Inn along the

Old Coach Road which climbs up eastwards (now the official coast path). This passes below the site of a Roman fort and signal station on Highveer Point and continues above Woody Bay to join a toll road leading to the Valley of the Rocks and Lynmouth. There are excellent views of the South Wales coast.

Lynmouth

Much of the old centre was damaged in the floods of August 1952. The Rising Sun Inn and cottages along Mars Hill above the harbour are among the oldest buildings. Smugglers are said to have used the Rising Sun as their meeting place, and R D Blackmore stayed here while collecting material for *Lorna Doone*. In 1812 the poet Shelley stayed in a cottage on the site of the present Shelley's Cottage Hotel, and Coleridge and Wordsworth also visited Lynmouth. The Memorial Hall, commemorating the flood of 1952, stands on the site of the old lifeboat station. In January 1899, in a heroic effort, the Lynmouth lifeboat was dragged overland to be launched at Porlock Weir to rescue a ship in distress. To explore the lighthouse or Foreland Point (where the smugglers' lookout waited) use the carpark on Countisbury Common east of Lynmouth (SS 754496). There is another path to Foreland Point from behind Countisbury church. To explore the Glenthorne Estate and visit the smuggling beach there, collect a free leaflet (giving a circular route) at the Tourist Information Centre at County Gate (SS 795487) which has a carpark and small exhibition. There is a tell-tale cellar below this little building!

Postscript

In 1857 the *First Annual Report of the Commissioners of Customs* stated:

> 'Smuggling is greatly diminished, and the public sentiments with regard to it have undergone a very considerable change. The smuggler is no longer an object of general sympathy or a hero of romance; and people are beginning to awaken to the perception of the fact that his offence is less a fraud on the Revenue than a robbery of the fair trader.'

Of course petty smuggling continued to some extent, and revived considerably during the period of austerity after the Second World War. Since then drug smuggling has become a major problem, and there have been numerous seizures in places associated with the free trade of 200 years ago – in Torbay in Devon, near Polperro and Sennen in Cornwall, at the port of Dover, in Poole Harbour, along the Essex marshes and even on Scottish islands and the west Wales coast. But if the traditional venues are still in use, the nature of recent smuggling operations is quite different. For a start, the sums of money involved are huge, and the smuggling networks worldwide. The power of the drug barons and the links with international crime have devasting consequences, particularly in Colombia. It is also said that some drug addicts are spending up to £1,000 a day on crack, and turn to crime to maintain their habit. Fortunately, opposition to the smugglers is also increasingly on an international scale, as can be seen from a few recent instances (four in October 1989 and three in July 1990, for example).

One of the largest hauls of cannabis resin (1,600,000 tonnes worth over £5 million) was captured by armed police off south-west England on 13th October 1989. The motor yacht *Rosy* had visited Morocco and then been under surveillance after leaving Gibraltar. The authorities of France, Spain and Gibraltar had all been involved in an operation which ended

The magnificant beach at Whitesand Bay, Sennen, where 300 or more men attacked Revenue officers guarding a huge cache of contraband, and right up to date, drugs were found in March 1990.

when the crew of four got into difficulties ten miles off Falmouth and radioed for help. Addresses in London were also searched in a back-up operation.

Two weeks later *The Times* reported three quite separate episodes. The first account was from Eindhoven in Holland, where a joint operation by Dutch and Belgian police arrested 16 people and claimed to have smashed a network engaged in smuggling marijuana from the Philippines to Britain via Hong Kong, the Soviet Union, Holland and Belgium. The authorities had been alerted when a smuggler was captured trying to sell the drug 'ecstasy'. The same day (October 28th) *The Times* reported that the Americans had built a jungle base in the upper Huallaga valley in Peru, the largest source of coca leaf for making cocaine, in an attempt to control the growing and processing of the drug. Using helicopters flying from a specially constructed airstrip, they succeeded in destroying 19 processing laboratories and 12 airstrips, and captured over 6,000 lb of cocaine paste. The American authorities were also struggling at this time to limit the flood of drugs entering the 189 country from Colombia. The third report concerned the largest recorded seizure of cannabis to date, with a street value now reported as over £60 million. Again this was the result of international cooperation, and the Honduran registered vessel *Altea* had been shadowed since leaving Holland. She was brought into Dover by two Customs cutters, where the drugs were discovered in the hold. Dover is now in the front line of the fight against drugs, and the value of these illegal imports to Britain totalled £244,700,000 in 1990.

A smaller but more dramatic episode took place in Kent in July 1990. The motor cruiser *Merulius*, registered at Portsmouth, was caught as the result of a three month operation involving the cooperation of British, French and Dutch Customs forces. The ship, with her crew of five, was shadowed as she sailed from Vlissingen in Holland, and the arrest took place at Kingsferry Bridge, Sheppey with help from a helicopter using a searchlight. Armed police fired a stun grenade as the vessel was boarded, and 60 kg of amphetamine sulphate (or speed) said to be worth £10 million was seized. Six other men (all British) were arrested at addresses in the London area. Speed is regarded as the poor man's cocaine, being easy to manufacture and cheap to buy, at a street price of about £4 per gram. Its increased use is probably linked to the popularity of acid house parties.

On the same day it was reported that two English teenage girls from the Midlands had been arrested at Bangkok airport in Thailand, and charged with trying to export over 67 lb of 95% pure heroin (valued at £4 million) on a KLM flight to Amsterdam. And a doctor from Edinburgh was fined £125 for trying to export seven grams of cannabis at Heathrow airport in his sporran. Jack Rattenbury would have appreciated that!

Appendix I

KEY DATES IN THE SMUGGLING STORY

1698 Act against Owling creates a landguard of Riding Officers

1702–12 War of the Spanish Succession

1706 Act of Union between England and Scotland

1715 Rebellion in Scotland under the Old Pretender

1717 Smuggling Act. Smugglers who refused to plead liable to transportation

1718 Hovering Act. Vessels under 50 tons liable to seizure if found loitering within 6 miles of the coast and laden with tea, brandy, silk etc

1721 Smuggling Act. Convicted smugglers to be transported for 7 years. Boats with more than 4 oars liable to confiscation and destruction

1724 Robert Walpole adds tea to items liable to Excise duty

1736 Inquiry under Sir John Cope takes evidence on smuggling

Smuggling Act increases penalties; severe fines for bribing officers, death for wounding or taking up arms against officers, transportation (if unarmed) for resisting arrest. Also an Act of Indemnity; a smuggler, even if in gaol, could have a free pardon if he confessed all and gave the names of his associates

1740–48 War of the Austrian Succession

1744 Threat of invasion from France

1745 Rebellion under Bonnie Prince Charlie

Parliamentary Inquiry into the tea trade; tea duty cut

Further penalties for those found loitering within 6 miles of the coast

1746 Battle of Culloden and final defeat of the Jacobites

Smuggling Act establishes the severest penalties. Death for running contraband, assembling to run goods or harbouring smugglers. Smugglers convicted of killing officers to be gibbeted. Collective fines on whole county for unresolved offences. Names of known smugglers published in the London Gazette; these men to surrender within 40 days or be judged guilty. £500 reward for turning in a gazetted smuggler

1756–63 The Seven Years War

1759 Tea duty raised again

1765 Isle of Man brought within Customs control

1767 First attempt to establish a Custom House on Jersey

1775–83 War of American Independence

1779 Smuggling Act, amending measures of 1746 Act and adding penalties for goods carried in vessels under 200 tons. Penalties for gaolers allowing smugglers to escape

1782 Act of Oblivion. Smugglers could redeem their crimes by finding men to serve in army or navy

1784 Prime Minister Pitt cuts tea duty from 125% to 12½%. Modifications to Smuggling and Hovering Acts

1793–1815 War with France, interrupted by short interval of peace March 1802–May 1803

1805 Customs control extended to Channel Isles

1809 New Preventive Waterguard created

1816 Control of Revenue cutters transferred to Admiralty

1817 Coast Blockade initially set up in Kent

1822 National Coast Guard established

1826 Further modifications to Smuggling Acts

1828 Customs control extended to the Scilly Isles

1831 Coastguard service replaces Coast Blockade in Kent and Sussex

1835 First steamer employed in the Preventive service

1844 Select Committee Report on the Tobacco Trade

1845 Sir Robert Peel removes duties on a wide range of items

1846 Repeal of the Corn Laws

1850 Last export duty (on coal in foreign ships) abolished

1853 Gladstone reforms the Customs service

Appendix II

GLOSSARY

Anker: A measure of spirits, generally 7½–8 gallons. Half anker barrels of approximately 4 gallons became the usual size for easy transport.

Bat: A long wooden stave used as a weapon by smugglers.

Boatsitter: A chief boatman in the Preventive Waterguard.

Coast Blockade: The preventive system in Kent & Sussex 1817–31.

Coastguard: (first called Coast Guard) The national preventive service established under Capt W Bowles, appointed 1822.

Coastwaiter: The Customs officer responsible for vessels from home ports.

Collector: The head of the Customs personnel at each port.

Comptroller: The Collector's deputy at the larger ports.

Cutter: A single-masted vessel, rigged like a sloop but with a running bowsprit.

Dragoon: A mounted soldier.

Exciseman: An officer responsible for assessing and collecting Excise Duty.

Flink Pistol: Used to flash a signal; in appearance like a starting gun.

Free trader: A smuggler.

Galley: A large open rowboat, typically propelled by up to 20 oars.

Geneva: Gin, also known as Hollands.

Hanger: A sword.

Huer: A man who kept watch for pilchard shoals.

Jacobite: A supporter of James II after his abdication, or of his son.

Landwaiter: The Customs official who supervised the unloading of ships from foreign ports.

Lugger: A vessel with four-cornered sails, rigged fore-and-aft.

Owler: Anyone smuggling wool out of England.

Pilchard palace or cellar: Where pilchards were stored and pressed for oil.

Preventive Waterguard: Preventive service established in 1809 covering whole country in 3 districts; patrols by cutters and small preventive boats.

Privateer: A privately-owned armed vessel holding a government commission to wage war on enemy ships.

Riding Officer: Officer in the Customs service appointed to patrol on horseback, initially to counter the owling trade.

Run: A successful landing of contraband.

Safe House: An inn or other building providing a recognised refuge for smugglers, usually for storage and stabling.

Sloop or Shallop: A small single-masted fore-and-aft rigged ship.

Sowing a crop: Sinking a raft of tubs in a marked position offshore.

Spout lantern: A signalling lantern made to send out a beam of light through a long spout attachment.

Tap: An unlicenced beer house.

Tide Surveyor: The Customs officer responsible for rummaging (searching) vessels anchored in port.

Tub: A wooden cask holding a ½ anker of spirits (approx. 4 gallons).

Wherry: A small open-decked sailing vessel with a very shallow draft, typically from Ireland.

Appendix III

THE CARTER FAMILY FIRM

Francis Carter married Annice Williams in 1736; they had ten children.
Those listed in capitals were involved in smuggling.

1. THOMAS 1737–1818. Had at least a passive interest in the trade, but was well enough off to own silver spoons and forks! Part owner of at least one vessel.
2. JOHN 1738–1803. 'The King of Prussia' and head of the family firm.
3. Frances 1739–44. Died in childhood.
4. Ann 1742–? Married RICHARD CHAMPION who became closely involved. Part owned at least three vessels.
5. FRANCIS 1744–1814. Part owner of at least one vessel, but later gave up smuggling and went to live at Rinsey.
6. Alse. Died in infancy.
7. HENRY or HARRY 1749–1829. Involved as owner, part owner or captain of various vessels. Also took part in the purchase and distribution of contraband. Gave up smuggling after his return from a French prison.
8. EDWARD 1751–? Listed as part owner of two vessels.
9. ROGER 1754–? Described as a mariner; part owner and captain of the *Phoenix* vessel.
10. CHARLES 1757–1803. Described as a merchant and having a small holding. Part owner of the *Friendship*; was the lander at Cawsand in 1788.

LICENSED PRIVATEERS OWNED BY THE FIRM DURING THE WAR OF AMERICAN INDEPENDENCE

Swallow 200 tons, 16 mounted guns, 26 swivel guns, crew of 60. Owned by John and captained by Harry in 1777; built at Bridport.
Phoenix 60 tons, 8 mounted guns and 10 swivels, crew of 50. Owned jointly by Roger, Edward and Richard Champion. Captained by Roger Carter in 1778.

Friendship 30 tons, 10 swivel guns, crew of 30. Jointly owned by John, Charles, Francis and Richard Champion; commanded by Francis Pearce.

Shaftesbury 200 tons, 16 mounted guns and 12 swivels, crew of 80. Owned jointly by John, Edward, Harry and Richard Champion. Commanded by Harry in 1780.

Phoenix (2) 150 tons, 20 mounted guns and 16 swivels, crew of 50. Commissioned 1781 and commanded by Ralph Dewen. Owned by John Carter, John Dunkin and Moses Simons.

A number of other vessels figure in the story, being owned or operated, legally or otherwise, by members of the family. One example is the *Revenge* which Harry commanded at Cawsand in 1788.

Ironically John Carter Richards, a descendant born in 1811, was drowned when he volunteered to assist the Coastguards while trying to rescue a wreck in Prussia Cove on 22nd March 1841.

Appendix IV

THE WILL OF HENRY CARTER

In the name of God Amen. I Henry Carter of Rinsey in the Parish of Breage and County of Cornwall, being in health of body and of sound and disposing mind, memory and understanding, but considering the uncertainty of life do make this my last Will and Testament in maner and form following; That is to say Whereas James Macculloch Senior of the Island Guernsey, with an intension of providing me bread has for several years past lent me sundry sums of Money without Interest thereon, and being afraid that my effects at the time of my decease may not be sufficient to indemnify him, and to avoid their being disipated I give and Bequeath unto the said James Macculloch for the affection I bear unto him after paying my lawful debts all my Effects wether in Goods, Chattles, Money, Plate, Jewells, Leasehold estates or Effects of any denomination whatsoever And I do hereby nominate and appoint the said James Macculloch Executor of this my last Will and Testament hereby revoking all former Will and Wills by me heretofore made In Witness whereof I have hereunto set my hand and seal this thirteenth day of July and in the Year of our Lord one thousand eight hundred and twenty six
Signed sealed published and declared by the above named Henry Carter the Testator as and for his last Will and Testament in the presence of us who have hereunto subscribed our names as Witnesses thereto at his request and in his presence and in the presence of each other

(Signed) George Carter   (Signed) Hen J Carter
Thos. Mitchell Jun.

I am indebted to Mr Peter Pool of Connor Downs for a copy of this will; the original is in Cornwall County Archives.

Bibliography

The best contemporary accounts of what took place are in the correspondence between the Board of Customs in London and the Collectors in the chief ports, the so-called Outport Letters. The originals are in the Public Record Office at Kew, but more convenient sources are the transcribed and edited versions preserved in the Customs and Excise Library in London. The main local newspaper collections are on microfilm. The *Exeter Flying Post* is at the West Country Studies Library in Exeter. The *Royal Cornwall Gazette* and the *Sherborne Mercury* are at the Cornish Studies Library in Redruth. Other useful collections are at the Institute of Cornish Studies at Redruth, The Royal Institution of Cornwall (including its journal, the JRIC) at Truro, and the Cornwall Record Office, also at Truro.

Chapter 1
Contemporary Sources
Cross, A L *Eighteenth Century Documents relating to the Royal Forests, the Sheriffs and Smuggling* New York, 1928
Exeter Flying Post
Report of the Select Committee of the House of Commons on the Tobacco Trade 1844
Other Sources
Chatterton E Keble *King's Cutters & Smugglers 1700–1855* London, 1912
Shore, Henry N *Smuggling Days & Smuggling Ways* London, 1892
Smith, Graham *Something to Declare* London, 1980
Teignmouth, Lord (Shore H N) & Harper, Charles G *The Smugglers* London, 1923
Williams, Neville *Contraband Cargoes* London, 1959
Wood, G Bernard *Smugglers' Britain* London, 1966

Chapter 2
Contemporary Sources
Outport letters of Dartmouth, Exeter & Plymouth
Rattenbury, John *Memoirs of a Smuggler* Sidmouth, 1837, reissued Newcastle, 1967
Other Sources
Bridger, J A D 'Cornish Smuggling' *JRIC 3 (NS) 1957–60* pp 24–31
Hippisley Coxe, Anthony D *A Book about Smuggling in the West Country 1700–1850* Padstow, 1984
Morley, Geoffrey *Smuggling in Hampshire & Dorset 1700–1850* Newbury, 1983
Smith, Graham 'The Great Anti-Smuggler' *Dorset County Magazine* 101 pp 3–18
Waugh, Mary *Smuggling in Kent & Sussex 1700–1840* Newbury, 1985
Williams, Neville *Contraband Cargoes* London, 1959

Chapter 3
Contemporary Sources
Exeter Outport Letters
Exeter Flying Post
Rattenbury, John *Memoirs of a Smuggler* Sidmouth, 1837, reissued Newcastle, 1967
Other Sources
Bush, Robin *The Book of Exmouth* Buckingham, 1978
Coxhead, J R W *Smuggling Days in Devon* Exmouth, 1956
Farquharson-Coe, A *Devon Smugglers* St Ives, 1975

Chapter 4
Contemporary Sources
Dartmouth Outport Letters
Exeter Flying Post
Other Sources
Coxhead, J R W *Smuggling Days in Devon* Exmouth, 1956
Hippisley Coxe, Anthony D *A Book about Smuggling in the West Country* Padstow, 1984
Wood, G Bernard *Smugglers' Britain* London, 1966

199

Chapter 5
Contemporary Sources
Dartmouth & Plymouth Outport Letters
Exeter Flying Post
Other Sources
Shore, Henry N *Old Foye Days Part II The Smugglers* 1907

Chapter 6
Contemporary Sources
Sherborne Mercury
Royal Cornwall Gazette
Other Sources
Bridger, J A D Report of lecture in *West Briton & Cornwall Advertiser* 22.10.1931
Bridger, J A D Reference notes in Royal Institution of Cornwall
Douch, H L Reference cards in Royal Institution of Cornwall
Keast, John 'Smuggling Days' *Old Cornwall* 1954, pp 182–5
Newcombe, Lisa *Smuggling in Devon & Cornwall* Norwich, 1975
Noall, Cyril *Smuggling in Cornwall* Truro, 1971
Noall, C Collection of notes and material in Royal Institution of Cornwall
Shapcott, E S 'A Little Looe Smuggling and a few Looe Ghosts' *Old Cornwall* 1928, pp 16–25
Shore, Henry N *Smuggling Days & Smuggling Ways* London, 1892

Chapter 7
Contemporary Sources
Falmouth Outport Letters
Sherborne Mercury
Royal Cornwall Gazette
Bridger, J A D (as in Chapter 6)
Douch, H L *Old Cornish Inns & their place in the Social History of the County* Truro, 1966
Mudd, David *The Falmouth Packets* 1978
Noall, Cyril *Smuggling in Cornwall* Truro 1971 and his notes in Royal Institution of Cornwall
Wood, G Bernard *Smugglers' Britain* London, 1966

Chapter 8

Contemporary Sources
Henry Carter's *Bond* of April 1799 in Cornwall Record Office, X634/62
Henry Carter's *Will* of July 1806 in Cornwall Record Office, X634/67 A 1&2
Penzance Outport Letters
Exeter Flying Post
Royal Cornwall Gazette
Cornish, John B (ed) *The Autobiography of Captain Harry Carter of Prussia Cove, A Cornish Smuggler* 2nd edition, 1900
Other Sources
Bridger, J A D 'Cornish Smuggling' *JRIC* 3 NS 1957–60, pp 24–31
Cunnack, E M 'The Carters of Rinsey. Their Forebears and Descendants' Typescript in Cornwall County Record Office X635
Hippisley Coxe, Anthony D *A Book about Smuggling in the West Country* Padstow, 1984
Noall, Cyril *Smuggling in Cornwall* Truro, 1971
Old Cornwall Vol 4 p 290 'How the Brandy came safe to Sithney'
Pollard, Frank 'Smuggler – Captain Harry Carter' *JIRC* NS V 1968 pp 324–381

Chapter 9

Contemporary Sources
Penzance Outport Letters
Royal Cornwall Gazette
Sherborne Mercury
Other Sources
Acton, Bob *Around Newquay: Landfall Walks Books 5* Truro, 1990
Bridger, J A D Extracts from 18th century Customs Books (Notes in Royal Institution of Cornwall)
Hippisley Coxe, Anthony D *A Book about Smuggling in the West Country* Padstow, 1984
Noall, Cyril *Smuggling in Cornwall* Truro, 1971
Opie, S A 'Smuggling Memories' *Old Cornwall* 1930 pp 30–31
Rendell, Joan *Hawker Country* Bodmin, 1980

Vivian, John *Tales of Cornish Smugglers* Truro, undated
Williams, Neville *Contraband Cargoes* London, 1959

Chapter 10
Contemporary Sources
Barnstaple, Bridgwater & Swansea Outport Letters
Exeter Flying Post
Sherborne Mercury
Other Sources
Farquharson-Coe, A *Devon Smugglers* St Ives, 1975
Hippisley Coxe, Anthony D *A Book about Smuggling in the West Country* Padstow, 1984
Smith, Graham *Smuggling in the Bristol Channel 1700–1850* Newbury, 1989

Index

INDEX

204

205

INDEX